The Leader in the Mirror

A Second Chance to Close the Gap

Eric J. Powell

The Leader in the Mirror
Copyright © 2015 by Eric J. Powell

ISBN: 978-0-9937951-3-8

All rights reserved. No portion of this book may be reproduced, stored in a retrieval system, or transmitted in any form or by any means—electronic, mechanical, photocopy, recording, or any other—without prior written consent from the publisher.

Unless otherwise marked, Scripture quotations taken from the HOLY BIBLE, NEW INTERNATIONAL VERSION®. Copyright© 1973, 1978, 1984 by International Bible Society. Used by permission of Zondervan Publishing House. All rights reserved.

onCUE©, the Societal Ecosystem©, CUE Leadership©, CUE Leadership Matrix©, Axis of Leadership©, and charts and graphs shown are copyright 2010 by CUE Foundation, Inc.

Author photo by Terry Dean of Creative Photo Arts

Cover design by Touch Publishing

Published by Touch Publishing
Requests should be directed to:
P.O. Box 180303
Arlington, Texas 76096
www.TouchPublishingServices.com

To connect with Eric Powell visit www.cueleadership.org

Library of Congress Control Number: 2014944280

Printed in the United States of America on acid-free paper

Many Thanks!

I offer special thanks to all who have touched, guided, and obliged me in bringing CUE Leadership to life; especially my family, friends, and colleagues who entered the "Huddle" workshops. I would be remiss if I did not mention my good friend, Jacques Smith, who was my test case for our leadership diagnostic tool, CUE 360. Their openness to expose themselves helped to refine the core part of our ministry. Many Thanks!

Scripture tells us that when a man finds a wife, he finds a "good thing and obtains favor from the Lord." I thank the Lord for my best friend, my muse, my "good thing" —my wife Tai. I thank you for all that you are. What a refreshing balance you are… I dedicate this book to you and our girls, Kennedy and Karson. I pray that the Lord covers us with His favor… ~ Me

CONTENTS

Foreword	i
Introduction	1
Chapter 1: Me-Now Culture	**3**
"Peter! Peter! Peter!"	
Chapter 2: The Model for Leadership	**17**
"He's going to be transformational."	
Chapter 3: Dysfunctional Leadership	**35**
"Ya be whatcha see."	
Chapter 4: Advocate Leadership	**53**
"I got Eric!"	
Chapter 5: Steward Leadership	**73**
"Are you being a good boy scout?"	
Chapter 6: Gatekeeper Leadership	**93**
"Uncle Bay ain't gonna kill me!"	
Chapter 7: Transformative Leadership	**113**
"So what?"	
Chapter 8: Chief Shepherd	**129**
"Can I make my mark?"	
Chapter 9: Transforming the Leader in the Mirror	**147**
"Who was this guy?"	
CUE Leadership Reference Charts	**173**
Author BIO and About CUE Leadership	**175**
Captured Moments	**179**

Foreword

What is transformation? What does it look like? How does it feel? How can we tell that what we observe and define to have been transformed or even transmorphed has truly undergone a change or modification in its molecular DNA, its very essence? Next to the miracle of life itself, there are few truly miraculous transformations that continue to capture our wonder and amazement. Take, for example, the butterfly; for it undergoes one of the most amazing metamorphic transformations known to mankind. In its simplistic way, this phenomenon of nature reminds us of the very essence of life itself, as we consistently and intrepidly search for who we are, why we are here, what is our purpose, or what are our purposes, and, like the butterfly, what beauty resides within us yearning to be set free to the amazement of the world?

We continue this life's journey searching for our true selves in a book, in a job, in our families, in our churches, mosques, cathedrals, and temples... everywhere but within that vast and most bountiful knowledge repository we will ever have—our own Spirit made in God's image. We hunger for just that kind of connection that will identify our place within this vast mosaic, as Victor Frankl's ageless classic on mankind's search for significance and relevance abides us with some direction regarding where to look. Consider the brilliant visionary artiste Michelangelo, as even he would gaze on what most certainly must have appeared to be but a huge, monolithic block of stone, yet he could see David within; yearning to be set free.

Might some of these analogies remind you of how it felt as a child to be totally free, unabashed, intrepid, and forever searching for a sense of liberation, immediately following our first breath, rolling around but then testing, and ultimately mastering, gravity as we took those first few steps. Although we had not yet learned to clearly articulate the sensation we had discovered, our sense of accomplishment most likely showed up on our faces as we probably had thoughts ranging from, "Oh yeah, watch me now." Or more exuberantly, "Look, Ma... no hands!" The sense of what we had discovered about ourselves was so invigorating that we just knew we had life all figured out as we then realized, often to our parents' exhaustion, that we had an intractable need for speed as we discovered that we could run... everywhere freely and even recklessly, ready to share these unique discoveries with the world.

Remember how it is to observe a child, or pictures and videos of ourselves, undergoing that amazing transformation and the exultation that served as evidence of things not seen—yes, faith even at that young age. My previous questions regarding transformation address neither an anomaly, an enigma, nor even a miracle in the making for we butterflies are already here, relevant, and significant. Life too often pressures us to look for ourselves in those trappings we hold so near and dear believing, albeit errant, that these things define us to the world looking in.

I can think of no better example of how the river that flows within us can expose our inner core, more often than not to our amazement, than this novella created by one that I've had the pleasure and honor to have known, admire, and observe as he frantically, sometimes recklessly, chipped away to discover the unique David that resided within himself. When I first met Eric Powell he was determined even back then to emulate Stephen Jobs' greatest achievement—"to make a dent in the universe!" I remain so very impressed with this young man who even in his late twenties to early thirties was testing the Universe for impact possibilities. I'll leave some of the more fascinating stories, anecdotes, and epiphanies surrounding Eric's God-called journey for you to discover as he shares his own transformation to inner discovery and awareness regarding the river that has run through his Spirit.

Many of Eric's accomplishments will astonish you—feats of strength, willpower, tenacity, and endurance as he walked the halls of some of the most prestigious corporations in the world all while still in his thirties. The athletic prowess that he nurtured, embraced, and refined throughout his life are even more of a testimonial to the many blessings and spiritual gifts that have fueled his success. Eric still, after so many years continues to "epiphanize" —my word—his life and its many lessons as it has administered some very difficult and often stressful tests well in advance of the lesson to be learned; not quite the model we are accustomed to as we studied our subjects in school. Eric's composite exposé has created a model that will truly help you to appreciate the intrinsic value of introspection and self-discovery as you seek to elevate your journey to an even higher level, upgrading your quality of that journey from coach to first class.

At risk of dating myself, I can recall a variety of shows some decades ago called "soap operas" that were designed to capture the essence of everyday life complete with its trials, tribulations, pain, and anguish. But, as I pause to reflect on but a few of the titles, *The Guiding Light*, *Search for Tomorrow*, *The Days of Our Lives*, *The Young and The Restless*, I used to think that these programs were more about discovering who we really were or yearned to be albeit under the obvious guise of selling laundry detergent. And one day it hit me... "soap"—what a metaphor for what the producers really wanted us to glean from each episode, as a model cleansing agent for the mind, as it were. Real transformation is indeed a cleansing experience, as well as being invigorating, provocative, morphogenic, often therapeutic, and always "nutritional" when the sustenance is God's Holy Word.

I know you'll enjoy, and even relate to, so many of Eric's transformational lessons in life, possibly even embracing many as your own. Enjoy and discover the wonder and beauty that flourishes within you!

Dr. Gerald Turner
Eric's Brother in Christ

INTRODUCTION

One of my favorite authors, Mark Twain, shared, "The two most important days in your life are the day you are born and the day you find out why." You definitely have experienced the first one. My first day almost did not happen, for I was breached during birth. Turned the wrong way, I seemed to have a mind of my own and wanted to do things my way. I thank God for delivering both me and my mom that important day. Mom was near death and barely survived. She fought hard for us. She may tell you that my "mind of my own" has had her worried ever since. Recently, I overheard Mom jokingly whisper to my wife, "God help me! I sometimes wonder where did that boy come from... if he even belongs to me?" I admit that I have been doing things my way most of my life.

The second day that Twain wrote about was about discovering one's God-given purpose; a calling, an election, a reason for being... The Lord may say the same as Mom because He tried to show me the other most important day early in my life, but I ran, did things my way, and got all turned around... breached before my new birth. Have you experienced your second most important day? I have. The Lord helped me discover my purpose; He birthed it out of me and used my breached position to close a gap that existed between Him and me. There is a gap in this generation's leadership. Many potential-filled men and women are in need of a catalyst to help them experience their own "second most important" day. I thank the Lord for not giving up on me and for giving me a second chance to get onCUE with His calling on my life. This book is designed to show you that your second chance is waiting. There are steps you can take to make significant strides on your leadership journey.

Romans 8:28-29 reads: "And we know that in all things God works for the good of those who love Him, who have been called according to His purpose." I pray this for you and for me in raising, inspiring, and equipping new leaders for the Lord's glory—the Leader in the Mirror. There are many books on leadership, purpose, accountability, faith, transformation, self-assessment, change management, and team building, but the question is what happens when all of those come together under the Lord's leadership? I'm not talking about a fad or "self-help." This is not a book on *how* you worship but *that* you worship; not a book to criticize but to shine some light in truth and love; not a book to tell you what to do

but provide a different lens to see things through; and not a book to focus on the mere symptoms of a problem but to identify the root of the problem. This is not a book about religion, but a testimony about having intimacy with, trying to get on one accord with, and getting new life with the Lord. This is not a book on project or employee management, directly, but a book to help the leader in the mirror to confront the realities...
- of the world... broken and scattered.
- of the need for transformation... in the world and in the mirror.
- of God's calling on your life... your God-given purpose.
- of your ability to lead in that purpose... get people to trust you and follow you.

For now, can I ask you to trust me and can I invite you to follow me... at least through my testimony? My testimony is about transformational leadership based in the Word of God. I admit that I have been doing things my way most of my life but have been observant of and influenced by many. In this book I highlight everyday leaders that have made a difference in me and in my life, and who testify to God's goodness.

I suspect through these pages you will laugh, smile, think, reflect, and cry. No matter your status, success, pains, failures, dreams, passion, job, vice, mistakes, fears, or circumstance, there is something for everyone, no matter the season of life. I pray that you look in the mirror and assess what type of leader you are, huddle at the breach, and become a catalyst yourself to close the gap in our society—get on purpose to lead where you are... get onCUE!

Chapter 1: Me-Now Culture

"Peter! Peter! Peter!"
—Football punt returner

There is no more exciting, dynamic play in football than the punt return. No other play can shift momentum, change the game, or energize a team and crowd in the blink of an eye. Think about it with me for a moment. Imagine the sound of the thump as the ball makes contact with the punter's foot. It ascends. Sense the odd silence as the crowd holds its breath, waiting to see what will happen. Feel the opposing team gain ground by running full-speed toward you. All the while, you must make the assessment of this oddly-shaped ball's flight—the direction, speed, and thread movements. Now position yourself accordingly, knowing that coaches look on expectantly to see if the team will execute the plan. What happens next will determine the flavor of the game.

Man, I can feel the excitement of the play as I picture it because I was a punt returner in college more than 20 seasons ago. I played for the mighty Gamecocks of Jacksonville State University (JSU) in Alabama.

No matter if the punt was flying long or short, had a high or low trajectory, was coming end-over-end, or in a tight spiral, my job was to catch the ball and get to the wall. The wall was made of my teammates who:

1. knew the game plan,
2. were prepared, and
3. knew their roles.

That play can work for you or work against you. I have been on both ends.

When it worked, the wall play was special, but if I mishandled the ball, if I did not get to the wall, or if one my teammates missed a block, the play was less dynamic. Lack of preparation, readiness, focus, toughness, execution, or knowledge would result in a gap in the wall. With a gap in

Chapter 1: Me-Now Culture

the wall, our opponents could easily converge out of their lanes and make a play. Even if opponents broke through the gap, I knew that if I could make the first one or two miss, we still had a fighting chance.

Now there were times when I would have to call for a fair catch or call, "Peter! Peter! Peter!" and let it roll away. Calling "Peter" alerted my team that they had to change their assignments from blocking to finding the ball quickly, because I was giving up on the play.

How is this relevant to leadership? I submit to you that it is quite relevant and more so today than ever before. Pick any story in the news, on Twitter, on Facebook, or even in your home, at work, or in church. Increasingly, the narrative of the story is about *less*ness: hopelessness, homelessness, defenselessness, cheerlessness, powerlessness, truthlessness, ruthlessness, mercilessness, heartlessness. And it all leads to faithlessness. Not only are the young and old of this generation broken by circumstance, shamed by failures, desperate for fulfillment, and starved for the true bread of life, we are scattered and exposed to the more of the same.

Why? Because there is a failure in leadership, and we need better and new leadership now. We need at least two types of leaders to turn the "lessnesses" around:

Shepherds: These transformational leaders are dynamic game changers who can lead the shift and work the plan to make the wall happen, and,

Gatekeepers: These leaders will mend the gaps and stand apost once the wall is built.

Too many leaders in our nations, communities, places of worship, and families are calling "Peter" instead of doing the hard work of building the wall. They call "Peter" immediately, allowing the ball to bounce and roll deep, deep into enemy territory; a wilderness filled with irreverence to God's power, dominion, love, wrath, and presence. They call "Peter" instead of solving issues, focusing on results, and providing true transformation. They call "Peter" instead of calling on God, our eternal source, and instead of standing in faith and catching the punt to give this generation a fighting chance.

A fighting chance against what? The shift off the axis is due to a shift in culture. Leaders are fighting against a scattered generation (not just the young, but the old as well) that tells us that the world is all about "me" and it is all about "me, right now." Have you ever heard someone ask the question, "What's that have to do with me?" It is a sentiment that is easy to say, easy to feel, and easy to adopt.

Too many of us are comfortable to sit idly by and declare, "That is not my problem," or we hang back in fear of not acting with political correctness. We are idle. I mean this in two ways.

The first is in the truest sense of idle, where we are either standing still in fear, standing with indifference to what is happening around us, standing in shame, or standing without purpose. When there were no punts to return or plays to run, I remember standing in the midst of all of those. I especially remember the feeling of standing idle during my very last college football game. The sport that I loved, that consumed me, and that defined me was over. And I did not finish my football playing career on my terms. In that last game I was already at about 160 all-purpose yards by halftime and had even reversed field to score (for the first time in college).

But my fortune took a turn on account of a concussion. The concussion was mild, but our head trainer, Coach Jim Skidmore, took me out of the game as he remembered a bad concussion I had two years prior. I never argued with a coach before, but I sure did that day. When arguing did not work, I pleaded my cause, for this was "my moment."

Coach Skidmore did not budge, and said something to the effect that he was thinking about my future. I screamed, "My future? This is about *now*! Let me finish it! Don't take this away, please!" I was so desperate that I tried sneaking back into the game, but was caught. Coach Skidmore took my helmet and sent it to the locker room. The second half of that last game was the longest and toughest I had to endure, as I stood idle on the sideline.

I felt I deserved to finish the game, and it was my injury not his, so it was my call to make. While standing on the sideline, mentally and emotionally I entered the wilderness. Players of any sport often talk about their wilderness moment. Yes, I had run a 4:38 in the 40-yard dash for an NFL scout the prior spring, but who was I kidding? With my size, history of injuries, and that concussion, I confronted a reality that my chance to play at the next level like my older brother did was a long shot. In the locker room after the game, I wept uncontrollably and I could not take my pads off. I was frozen, idle, and fearful, for it was the last time

Chapter 1: Me-Now Culture

that I would suit up. I felt a major part of me die that day. Because I refused to remove my pads, my coaches sent for reinforcement—Sarah J. Powell, my mother. I can still picture her face as she rounded the corner into our locker room. As she approached, she blocked out the light as I turned and looked up.

With a confused and worried look on her face, Mom asked, "What's wrong, baby?"

I just said, "It's over... life is over."

She latched on to my words and repeated them quite sternly, "Life is over? How can you say *life is over*? Look at what you accomplished. Did not people tell you that you were too small to play college football like your brothers? Did you not only play as a starter, but win a national championship? Are you going to graduate?"

In between those questions, I mustered three, "Yes, Ma'ams."

She went on to say, "So if you proved people wrong, you have a ring, and will have a degree, why are you crying and hanging your head? Baby, you have to start another chapter and ask God what that is." Then, with a more forceful tone she instructed, "Dry your face, take off your pads, take a shower, get dressed, and come out with your head up and a smile on your face. Do it not just for yourself, but for yo'r nieces and nephews. They out there waiting for you."

Looking back, I was calling "Peter." When Mom asked me those questions in the locker room, she knew at that moment I had no *purpose*. I had defined my whole being, my identity, on something fleeting—something other than God. The Lord used her words to energize me and shift me away from a moment of idle weakness. Purposelessness and identity-lessness coupled with shame blinded me like the sun or stadium lights would when I did not have on eye black. The glare forced me to call "Peter" on life. I was blinded in that moment by sorrow, fear, anger, failure, indifference, circumstance, and by my own self. Football was my outlet and my god, and the end to the season just exposed the depth to which that was true. But God used Mom to take the glare away of my self-imposed cheerlessness, hopelessness, powerlessness, faithlessness—my *less*nesses. My lessnesses fed my own idleness.

Ironically, a similar idleness parallels what we see in today's culture—our "Me-Now culture." More destructive than personal idleness, the "Me-Now" culture manifests itself as more than just an argument with a coach. The notion that life is about "Me" and that I want what I want "Now" tears at the fabric of society and puts us in conflict with our ultimate coach—God. Me-Now culture is evident in the attacks on families, on God in the public forum, and on truths that we are supposed to hold dear on Sundays. Unless there is an emotionally-charged event [such as a police shooting, school shooting, a senseless tragedy, a public outcry, a personal tragedy (such as the end of one's football career), or Ferguson MO, Trayvon Martin, Murrysville PA, Donald Sterling's scandal or any of the other travesties on our world], that leaves us victimized by circumstance, we remain paralyzed, inactive, sluggish, slow, still, frozen, immobile, at rest. Like I was in that locker room, today's Me-Now culture is I.D.L.E.

Irreverence

I was irreverent to God's power, dominion, presence, love, and to His wrath. In that locker room I did not revere Him, even though I was the one who led our team chapel service before that very game and the games before. I forgot that God is omnipresent, omniscient, omnibus, omnipotent, and omnieternal. As such, I got "beside myself" and was blinded by the light of my own brilliance. I wondered if God was around, forgetting that everything is in His presence. Instead of throwing up my finger to Him when I scored, I picked up the new trend of "Xing" the other team out. (In doing this I was breaking the rules because our Hall of Fame Coach Bill Burgess did not tolerate end zone celebrations.)

I had forgotten that the Lord had given me some uncommon and amazing gifts to play this game. How many 5'6", 165-170 pound football players with a 40-inch vertical, a bench press of 400 pounds, and a squat of 600 pounds were there on this earth? The Lord knew better than to make me tall like my brothers, for I may have been unbearably arrogant and pompous and lack the tools that made me different. I had what it took, according to JSU's late president Dr. Harold MaGee. At the end of any talk or speech, he would share, "You got to have it here, here, and here." He would point to his head, heart, and stomach respectively, as he said it. He meant that we had to have the mind for clarity, the heart to try, and guts/grit to persevere. I believed that I had that to play well at that level. I use that imagery today in the same way as Dr. MaGee did, but I end it with: "but it starts here" as I point to our eternal and unchanging

Chapter 1: Me-Now Culture

source—God Almighty. He covered me, and initially I only revered Him during chapel, for show. God remains in control, no matter how smart, how enlightened, how rich, how advanced, or how *[add your own]* you become.

Dependence

The second component that keeps us idle is having dependence on or being anchored in things other than God. To know if you are in this danger, let me ask: In times of joy or in times of pain, on what do you initially depend? Who or what do you turn to first for answers? Your answer reveals your first filter in your decision-making process. Recognize it or not, you have a consistent first step in your decision-making process. Your compass will go to whatever you have set as your personal "true North." This could be yourself, something in the world (friend or vice), or to a doctrine other than God's. To not be idle, you must set your true North heavenward.

We all have areas of life in which we want to grow. This could be in our family, wealth, status, power, or influence, for example. My mother and father taught us the importance of being there for each other, but we also learned how to take personal responsibility. Each of us had to do his or her part on simple things such as baiting our own hooks, speaking for ourselves, and taking all of our "own swings." Let me explain.

Growing up, we played baseball a lot. We used community equipment supplied partly by Mt. Zion Missionary Baptist Church in my hometown of Greenville, Alabama, and partly by the community coach, Mr. Buddy. Everyone got a chance to play somewhere on the field, no matter what their skill level or age. When younger players were at bat, we had a rule that allowed someone older to take their last swing for them. We called it, "taking their last." I would nearly always have my brother Jody take my last. After two strikes, I would stand to the side, out of the batter's box, while Jody took my last swing. Then, when he hit the ball, I would run the bases. Everyone allowed this rule... except my Dad. Dad saw what we were doing one day and stopped the game. Still dirty from work and smelling of a mixture of diesel, oil, and chipped wood, he walked up, took the bat from Jody and gave it back to me. Then he said, "Don't ever let anyone bat for you."

I asked, "But what if I strike out?"

He replied in his frank and shrewd way, "Then ya just strike out. Then ya tried't again. You gotta learn for yo'self. You can do it."

Pops believed in us looking out for one another, being our brothers' keepers, but this was different. And he was right. If I had not taken the swings, I would have been looking for Jody to bail me out; to be my cushion and to provide a soft landing every time. Jody would have been a crutch and I would have been in continual need of his nourishment—dependent on his swing, not mine.

Nourishing and caring for self and others calls for the right sustenance. Depending on the wrong type of substance keeps us thirsty, hungry, or standing on the side for things that are neither filling nor sustaining. I would have found myself looking for help to bait my hook or leaning on the athletic laurels of local legends (my brothers), standing in the government cheese and powdered milk line (which I did with my mother during rainy weeks), or suckling on my mother and sisters for godly counsel and for grace. One of my former trainers shared it best when I polled fellow Gamecocks on what a "champion" was. He said: "Pull Your Own Wagon."

> "Everyone had a job to do and was expected to do it full speed! No matter who you were: player, coach, trainer, manager, you worked hard and pulled the wagon.
>
> There were no riders. We held each other to a higher standard on and off the field. No matter if we were in season or off season we always talked about getting to the championship game, never being satisfied with a "good" season. We always wanted to be great. Thanks to all my Gamecock family for letting me be a part of this journey and I appreciate how each of you have helped each other on our journey."

I now realize in that locker room, my growth was feeble and fleeting, for I was not pulling my own wagon with the Lord. I was depending on things other than Him for grace. Is your past, present, and future tied to the umbilical cord of the grace of man or the grace of God? Ask yourself honestly: What are you dependent upon?

Loyalty

Misplaced loyalty also contributes to our idleness. Loyalty is

Chapter 1: Me-Now Culture

misplaced when we follow something (or someone) blindly to justify our own happiness, pleasures, or circumstance. This kind of loyalty does not preserve things that are sacred, honorable, holy, or that are bigger than we are.

Misplaced loyalty can become clearly evident when it comes to politics. My politics are little different than the "We seek change for the sake of change" mindset. I have never been a democrat or republican, conservative or liberal, or anything in between. I do have conservative leanings, but I am neither a bandwagon jumper or a "yellow sheet" guy.

During election time, local politicians would make their rounds through our rural Mt. Zion community. We took the service and privilege to vote seriously; So seriously, community leaders would hand out a yellow sheet with all the candidates that the community supports. It was a straight democratic ticket. One year I ruffled some feathers. Now, I'm not saying I did not like the Democrat candidate, I was not on board with being told what to do. Plus, I played little league baseball and hung out with the son of one the candidates on the opposite side of the ticket. Why would I not vote for him? Imagine the gasps and the side conversations when I refused to take one of the yellow sheets. Yes, I was a little dramatic and smart-alecky when I said, "I don't need one of those. I vote for who I want."

One elder of our community murmured to another, "He is smart but disloyal. We have to watch him."

Well, over the years, I have been accused of being disloyal to my race, or a disgrace to my ancestors for questioning leaders, especially black leaders and political candidates who happen to be Democrats. It has been a transformation to what I hold true now. I have not been called "Uncle Tom," but as long as they don't call me "Sambo" (the loyal servant at all costs), I will be OK.

You must ask yourself: Are you so loyal to a cause that you are blinded? Whom do you serve? Why? Are you trying to serve two masters? To whom are you accountable? Are you talking out of both sides of your mouth when you talk about the Lord and then when you talk politics?

Entitlement

Entitlement, or when you feel that world owes you something, is the "E" in being I.D.L.E. As the saying goes, "I'm gonna get mine." We seem to show a level of impatience or unwillingness to wait our turn or to take on a less desirable role until it's "our time." We want to win, now, at all costs. The truth is: you cannot win every time. That was a hard lesson for me, and I learned it the hard way through college sports. Up until 1992, the year of our national championship, I had seldom, if ever, experienced a losing season in team competition—baseball, track, basketball, weightlifting, football, and even tournaments for mathematics, English literature, and the arts. Yes, I competed in academic tournaments as well as athletics.

After climbing the Division II mountain and reaching the national championship for the second year in a row, we won it. The feeling of winning a championship cannot be put into words. It was short-lived, for in the following year, we moved up to Division I-AA and lost many games over the next two years. Some were close and some not so close to the likes of Kurt Warner at Northern Iowa and Steve Air McNair at Alcorn State. I soon realized that I did not know how to lose, how to deal with failure, or how to control my emotions. I felt that I was owed something and that I was entitled to win. This was a hard lesson, but now I know that season of life had a purpose. The related short-term gratification feeds the "Now" side and makes us impatient, impairing our ability to have a long-term, generational view. A sense of entitlement feeds, fosters, and funds the emerging inequality doctrine that leads our politics, government, product branding, corporations, marriage, race, healthcare, glass ceilings, churches, little league sports, etc. This doctrine is strategic and smart because it feeds self and flesh, justifies our feelings, and ignites protest, all the while maintaining the veil of political correctness and Me-Now over all that it weds.

Ask yourself: Is this life about you or me? Are you second or getting yours? Do you feel that you are owed something?

Throughout Scripture, the Lord calls us to be one-to-another. That relationship is characterized by togetherness—love one another, encourage one another, and build up one another... be a brother's keeper. This is critical to us now more than ever, as the entitlement culture is driving more people to claim they are being victimized by their circumstances. Victimization is at the root of the Me-Now culture. When you make yourself a victim you also feel you are owed or entitled

Chapter 1: Me-Now Culture

to something to make up for it.

Victimization is moving from serving family, communities, nation, and others to operating in a whelm of fear. We get the "grasshopper syndrome," named after the ten of the twelve spies that Moses sent into Canaan. Even though God told them they would succeed in fighting their enemy, they allowed what they saw in the land reduce their confidence in their abilities, even though they had God Himself on their side! They became victims. Ten of the spies said they were like grasshoppers, as compared to the "giants" in Canaan. Idle in fear of losing the popular vote, Moses disobeyed the Lord and lost his moment to walk into the Promised Land. The chance passed him, and he and the people wandered the wilderness for another forty years. He did not take his chance.

The victimization mentality makes an excuse for everything. If there is one thing that sports teaches us, it is that there are no excuses! I heard that from my family and coaches—from Coach Gene Allen to Coach Bill Burgess. For Coach Burgess the oils of "no excuses" seeped through the pores of this old-school, fair, hard-nosed, but loving, coach. He led JSU to three Division II National Championship title games in a 4-year span, including his final win in 1992 with us. He is a Hall of Famer. In 1991, the title game was the only game we lost. In 1989, before my time, our Gamecocks lost a 3-0 heartbreaker, in the snow, to a team that JSU beat 35-7 a few weeks back in the regular season. This was devastating for that team, who were perhaps the best in JSU's history. A couple of years later, the NCAA forced the opposing team to give up their 1989 title. Apparently, the opponent had more than 90 players on scholarship, while the NCAA rule only allowed 65 players to be on scholarships. So the NCAA assumed that the title and trophy rightfully belonged to JSU with Coach Burgess. When the NCAA came to the University to present our 1992 title trophy, story has it that the NCAA brought along the 1989 trophy as well. Coach Burgess refused it by simply saying, "They had 11, and we had 11."

To him, it did not matter if the opponent had more scholarships. That would be an excuse, because he put his best 11 players on the field against their best 11. Coach Burgess could have agreed, accepted the trophy, played the victim, and claimed they were at a disadvantage when they lost.

But what would his accepting the trophy have told us? He would not have been the leader that he wanted us to be—showing us how to properly respond to challenges, circumstance, or disadvantages. 1989 was not JSU's season, and it was over. Just like in the locker room my season was over. Was my God so small, where I fell victim to every ailment or shortcoming that placed me at a disadvantage? Was God so small He could not fix my problem? Could He not give me a new season or a new chapter? Could He not give me purpose?

Add the "V" of victimization to the letters in I.D.L.E. and rearrange them, you get the word "devil." Satan is the true author of confusion. He has a purpose in severing us from eternal fellowship with God. If "Satan talk" scares you off from our dialogue I understand, because it once scared me too and had me confused. Accept it or not, Satan was orchestrating his greatest trick on me and was not lifting a finger to do it. I was doing his job for him.

He was that glare that took my eyes off the punt. As a good friend and pastor shared, "Satan came after Jesus. He is not scared of you?"

Satan's was the voice of the high school booster who took the time at an awards banquet just to say, "I am glad you are smart because you won't play college football like your brothers." Satan loved to help me find myself on the opposite end of God; in confusion or in division. I was divided against God because I was focused on "Me" and "Now" and thought I was the exception to the rule.

The reality is that we often remain idle in both senses. I.D.L.E.ness coupled with division creates gaps in the wall. These gaps put the play, the game, the season, and the entire future generations at risk. Our Me-Now culture contributes to the gap, but there is an element at the root: failure of leadership. Leaders are calling "Peter," making excuses to justify behaviors, sticking to the popular or philosophical narrative, and causing gaps that are failing this generation and the next.

This failure happens because of one of two reasons:

1. Incompetence

Some leaders are simply not ready, not equipped, or not skilled in what they are leading.

Have you ever witnessed a person in a leadership role who was disruptive and dysfunctional? This person creates so much chaos, you question how he or she got the role to begin with. If you have not experienced one, bless you. Have you ever been under the guidance of someone who was transparent and shallow? Incompetent leaders focus more on themselves and on issues that are inconsequential to actually accomplishing real goals. Their ineptness prevents any progress from happening. They are toxic.

Toxic leadership can happen anywhere: homes, churches, businesses, the government—anywhere! Pick a side of the aisle politically, and there is the same venom; a viral toxin of being "disagreeable" that exists on Capitol Hill and, sadly, throughout our country. Economically, there are failures of leadership in corporate America.

When a leader is in a role that he or she is ill-equipped and incompetent for, they will often surround themselves with their own "amen corner" or supporters who are just as incompetent, and who are willing to go along with whatever is being fed to them. Incompetent leaders often get into their position because they are dynamic enough to appear that they know what they are doing, but we need to look more closely at what's underneath to see if they truly have the skills to get the job done.

2. Imprudence

An imprudent leader is one who is readily able to make unethical, immoral, irreverent, and unholy decisions. I believe that incompetence can be trained in most cases, but can imprudence? Imprudent leaders either make decisions that have the potential to harm people, or they will make personal decisions that put themselves and others in dangerous situations. This includes crack-smoking mayors, men of the cloth on the hustle, and leaders passing laws that allow the moral fabric of society to change for the worse. A good friend and regular guest on my onCUE! Radio Show put it best, "The church gave the world order; the world did not give the church order. The world just perverted the order that it was given. The perverted order that the world uses, the church has to allow that to stay with world."

Imprudent leaders have passion laced with the toxin of self, or of the world. I have seen it time and time again in the firms I have worked for and the firms in which I have served as a management consultant.

Imprudence cannot be changed without a transformation. It cannot be separated from goodness of God. Do you disagree? "Do not be deceived, my beloved bretheren," as James 1:17 tells us, "Every good thing given and every perfect gift is from above, coming down from the Father of lights, with whom there is no variation or shifting shadow." This goes for leadership, too. It is time to turn the tide and shift the momentum from our Me-Now culture. It is time to change the game and to get more people in the game.

How do we change the game? You might be wondering: "How do I lead people in the Me-Now culture who subscribe to this perverted order of thinking? How can I make a difference in someone's life if I am not their boss, not their sibling, or not their commanding officer? Can I make an impact if I have no formal authority over someone? Especially those in the Me-Now culture?"

There are political, economic, social, and educational changes that are warping the fabric of our society and that are shifting nations, communities, places of worship, our families, and our children off our collective axis. The decisions we make today impact the future for our children, their children, and generations after. Is "Now" your purpose? Or is the leader you see in the mirror standing in the gap?

The key to transformational leadership begins in two places. The first place is Scripture. Ecclesiastes 1:9 reads: "That which has been is that which will be, And that which has been done is that which will be done. So there is nothing new under the sun."

This means everything that is happening in the world has happened before in some form or fashion. While the environment, technology, culture, and transportation modes have evolved and changed, God's Word continues to be the only constant, eternal, unchanging source for answers; including our models of leadership.

The second place transformational leadership begins is with the leader you see when you look in the mirror. In Matthew 22:14 Jesus shares, "Many are called but few are chosen." Many of us hear the call of God, but only a few respond because they are the only ones who are truly hearing. Do you understand that there is a higher calling on your life? What is your purpose? Are you leading others with purpose? Are you willing to take a good look at the leader in the mirror? We are not

Chapter 1: Me-Now Culture

talking about "self-help," but rather being "God-led"—a life-long journey with the Lord.

Using Scripture and a commitment to develop the leader in the mirror, God can use you to be transformal in all facets of life—politically, economically, socially, and educationally. He has raised transformational leaders—Chief Shepherds—in the past. I pray that He will again, and I pray that includes you. When you declare that you will catch the ball whenever possible, call "Peter" only when absolutely necessary, and give up the I.D.L.E.ness that tempts you, only then will you change the game, close the gap, and cut the umbilical cord on the Me-Now culture. The only question is: who, what, or where is the ultimate model for the leader in the mirror?

Chapter 2:
THE MODEL FOR LEADERSHIP

"He's going to be transformational."
—Patron at the Renaissance Hotel, St. Louis, MO

In the fall of 2008, I was in St. Louis guiding a client through a process to strengthen their governance policies and procedures on capital spending. This client experienced major cost overruns in spending to the tune of millions of dollars. Our team initially found that the major violations were from a few bad actors who circumvented the budgeting, procurement, and approval processes, simply because they had the power to do so. But as we uncovered more, we found that almost 70% of the dollars spent were non-purchase order items; meaning there was almost no transparency on the majority of the company's spending. Imagine trying to get a client to confront a reality when they do not want to change. The only tool we had was their data. It was a challenge. The client scolded and embarrassed us at our first group workshop because we failed to revise a policy document. Our project lead tried to throw us (the rest of the team) under the bus in the meeting. He tried playing the "plausible deniability" card. Although I was the low man on the team, I called him to a private room and had a one-on-one to implore him that what he was doing was not teamwork, that it was embarrassing, and that he was not gaining favor with the executives, but rather showing them that he could not be trusted. A few on the client's team already did not trust him, even to the point where the client asked me not to bring him to meetings. That was a tough message to carry, which caused some issues and touchy team dynamics.

My time there was not all issue-filled. I was in St. Louis after all, where I could enjoy the great architecture, great food, great people, and a great baseball stadium. I stayed at the Renaissance Hotel most of the time during that project. It became a routine for me to arrive at the client by 7 or 7:30 A.M., work until 6:30 P.M., return to the hotel to change, eat dinner around 7:30 P.M., return to the hotel around 9, work until about 11:30 (while jazzed up on cappuccino), pray, and then retire

Chapter 2: The Model for Leadership

to bed around midnight after a shot or two of single malt whiskey. That was my life as a Booz management consultant from Monday to Thursday every week.

I wrapped the project up during the last week in October 2008. One evening, I arrived at the hotel and sensed something was different. The main elevator banks were blocked by men in bulky suits wearing ear pieces. They told me to use the other elevator bank, because the main elevators were down for routine maintenance. I thought that was strange, as I had been there for a few months and hadn't witnessed anything like that before. I used another elevator, and went upstairs to freshen up. That particular night, we had decided not to eat as a team. I had my own plans to go to my favorite tapas restaurant a few blocks over. When I returned downstairs, the energy in the lobby was palpable. There were more people, more men in bulky suits, more phones, and lots of cameras. *What was going on?* I wondered.

I decided to hang around for a bit. I spotted an open table in the lobby and sat down to observe. A group of ladies asked if they could sit with me, as they too seemed to be hanging around waiting to see what was happening.

I asked them, "What is going on?"

A woman in her forties responded, "You don't know?"

I asked, "Know what?"

She said, "Obama is staying here."

That explained the men in bulky suits (secret service with vests), the closed elevator bank (protecting and controlling the floors), all the people (media, staff, and supports), and the energy. At the time, Senator Obama was like a rockstar, blazing an unexplored trail.

I called Tai (my wife) and told her about Senator Obama. She was excited and encouraged me to position myself for conversation, to shake his hand, or at least to take a picture to send to her mom, Mother Trish, who was an active volunteer in the Chicago area for his campaign. My mother was of the same mindset. They both hung up the phone with me disappointed because my politics were a little different. I was in a dilemma that voting year. I did not agree with a lot of what Senator Obama said and stood for, and I was not going to cast a vote just because he was black, even if he had vision. But then again, how could I *not* go in the ballot booth and cast a vote for a black man, after all the generations before me had endured? I agreed more with Senator McCain's political ideas, but I refused to vote for a career politician, especially one with no vision. I believe career politicians are a part of our country's problem.

Like a good management consultant would approach a corporate quandary, I questioned the ladies sitting with me. I asked, "What is it about Obama that has you so excited?"

A 40-something year old black lady answered, "He is going to change things."

I followed up, "Help me with that. He's going to change what to what?"

No answer.

A 50-something year old white lady filled the silence by saying, "He is a great speaker."

I said, "Yes, absolutely. His voice seems anointed."

Then, a lady in her late 20s shared, "He is a great leader."

I turned to her quickly and asked, "What has he led? Help me." At this point, I sensed their cheery mood was changing, but I was seriously trying to understand.

The first black lady asked, "Are you secret service or something?"

Another black woman in her 30s replied, "No, he is a Republican! A black one at that!"

It seemed that I outstayed my welcome, even though they had joined my table.

I responded, "I am neither Democrat nor Republican. I honestly want to know why the excitement."

I assume they believed me because one of the black ladies finally said it: "He is gonna be transformational."

That word set my spider senses off. I said, "Now, you *have* to tell me about that. How do you know? How would anyone know?"

I thought the ladies were going to kick me out of my own spot, but I was saved by a commotion from the back of the hotel. There he was, the next President of the United States. Senator Obama walked in the midst of young secret service agents, looking tired on the last leg of the campaign. The place exploded with cheer. I have been in some loud places, but this blew them away. He slowed his walk, put one hand up, and shouted out, "Hey ev'rybody. How's ev'rybody doing?"

A few shouts came from the crowd. Then he called out, "Good

Chapter 2: The Model for Leadership

night!" and proceeded to the elevator. I said goodbye to my unwitting focus group. My spider sense, no, my *spirit*, was not settled. So, I went to my room, ordered room service, and opened my Bible. The Lord led me to the book of Nehemiah. For the next 18 to 24 months I stayed in Nehemiah. Morning and night I studied—asking the same questions that I asked the ladies at the hotel, plus more. I dissected that book just as any consultant would before writing an action plan. Then I began to write, tell the story, and paint the picture of a transformational leader using this man Nehemiah as my model. This journey started for my own edification, but morphed into the core of what CUE Leadership is all about—the Lord's brainchild, but my calling and my purpose.

What is leadership? Everyone has a different definition and uses varying words to describe leadership. Words like: inspirational, commanding, presence, in-charge, conductor, boss, charismatic, or whatever comes to your mind. No matter the connotation, someone in leadership is concerned with two things—Can I get you to:

1. TRUST me and,
2. FOLLOW me (Be a DISCIPLE)?

True leadership builds trust and discipleship, which are the Axis of Leadership. There are varying degrees of how effectively a leader does either. Too often, we label leaders as transformational by the *perceived* change they have been a part of or based on their ability to deliver a great speech. But transformational leadership is really the ability to garner trust and discipleship that is purposeful and foundational.

Most of today's visible leaders have self-imposed weights of gamesmanship and philosophy that scale back their ability to be transformational. Misguided gamesmanship and hardened philosophy impedes purposeful and foundational change that the nation and future generations need. Today's viral politics have no interest in elevating the hearts, minds, and spirits of people. Rather, the focus incites an ill-informed mass or creates victims based on ideas and positions that are not their own. We need more Nehemiahs—Shepherds—to change the game and close the gap created by the Me-Now culture.

As we identify various types of leadership and analyze them against Scripture, I will refer to the Leadership Matrix©. You see that trust and discipleship are at the axis of the matrix. We will fill in the matrix and highlight the strengths and/or weaknesses for each type of leader. Wherever you find yourself along the way, my prayer is that God will show you through these pages how you can move toward being a leader who is transformational; a leader like Nehemiah.

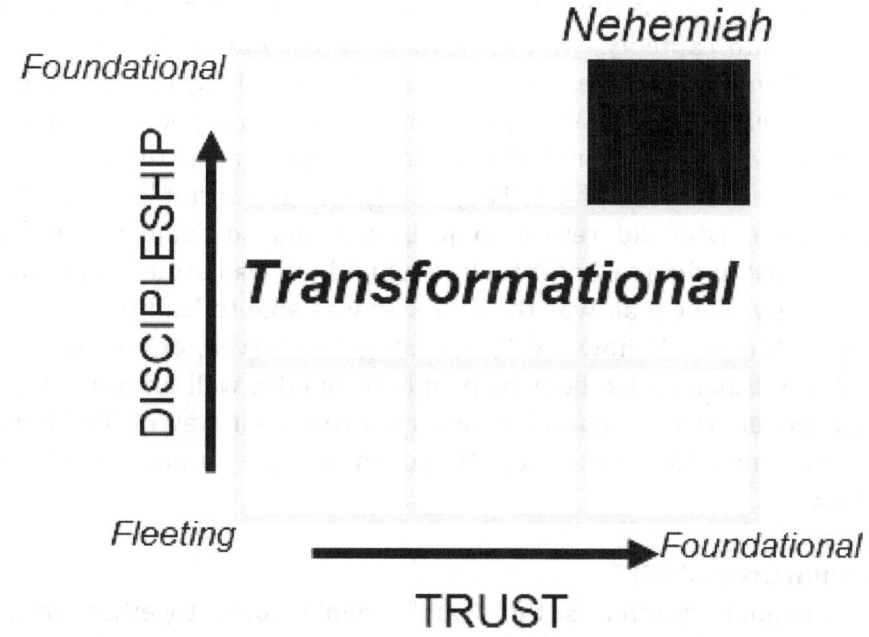

Why Nehemiah? Some have asked me, "Why didn't you choose our Lord and Savior Jesus as your leadership model?" The answer is simple: We, as sinful human beings, cannot attain His type of transformation or what He accomplished—not just his ability to lead, but His purpose from the Father. I can only seek to be *like* Him. I dare not compare myself or ask the leader in the mirror to compare him- or herself to the Great I Am, who is One with the Father, begotten not made, fulfilled the Scriptures, died on the cross for all sin, conquered death, resurrected on the third day, gives new life through Holy Spirit, and will return to reign forever. Comparing ourselves to Him is, in my opinion, irreverent.

Nehemiah's story provides us a specific situation in which we can examine and analyze his actions. The basis of the examination is not

Chapter 2: The Model for Leadership

from an academic or ideological viewpoint, but from my personal testimony. I was called to ministry while walking alone to Sunday school when I was ten years old. But, like many of us do, I ran from God for a long time. I thank Him for not giving up on me.

If you've never read Nehemiah's story, now would be a good time to pause, look it up in your Bible, and give it a read. The condensed version of the story is this: In 605 B.C. the Babylonians began to take the Israelites into captivity. They took them to Babylon to live. Jerusalem and the Temple were destroyed in 586 B.C. The Babylonian captivity lasted 70 years, to fulfill God's judgment on the Jewish people. When the Israelites were released and allowed to leave Babylon to return "home," many of them stayed behind. They had gotten comfortable where they were. Those who did return to Jerusalem did so disheartened and uninterested in doing what it took to rebuild the wall around their once beloved city. Nehemiah was the one who was able to lead the way and get the job done. So how did Nehemiah get a starved, exiled, doubtful, desperate, isolated, disobedient people to build a wall around ancient Jerusalem, effectively rebuilding and restoring their way of life? Here's how: Nehemiah CUE'd them up. He got the people on one accord with God's will.

Common Ground (C)

Common ground is the "why" people come together. At the opening of the book of Nehemiah, Jerusalem was in ruins. There were major gaps in the wall. Protective gates were non-existent. Nehemiah, who had heard of the state of his beloved city, called upon God to help him get to Jerusalem safely in order to lead its restoration. When Nehemiah got to Jerusalem, he knew he had to begin by finding common ground with the exiles. He reminded them that each of them had a share in Jerusalem. Each one had an historic right to the city and each had a claim in its future. Nehemiah connected his own life and his testimony with their plight, their needs, and their hopes. He showed that he empathized with their condition of shame and ruin, for he was starting from the same place. Finding common ground is a simple concept but will be the most difficult to perform if your audience does not connect with you.

Leaders who are most effective in finding common ground are the ones who can empathize with their audience. Being able to say, "I am just like you. I have been where you are," is powerful. More often than not, leaders who cannot empathize with their audience have to dive deeper for that connection by either understanding, relating, or sympathizing.

"I understand where you are." — The leader takes the audience to a common reference point in his/her life when the leader felt the same way that the audience is feeling now.

"I can relate to where you are." — The leader takes the audience to a reference point that impacted someone the leader knows.

"I can sympathize with you." — The leader attains sympathy from the audience with his/her own story or plight.

Think about a leader you respected but who could not empathize with you. They probably found common ground by walking you through one of those means. President Bill Clinton was and is a master at this. If you get a chance to listen to him speak, pay attention to the common ground technique he uses.

However, there is a misconception that finding common ground is enough, or that having common ground is leadership. We hear leaders, especially political ones, state: "we managed to find common ground," when seeking resolution on a matter, but then nothing else happens. When common ground cannot be found is often because the leader is focused on himself or herself. We do what is reasonable instead of what is right; we serve self rather than serve others. We satisfy the masses at the expense of our direct supporters. We allow ourselves to be guided by voice of the polls versus voice of unintended consequences. We are guided by the election cycle instead of the generational cycle. We treat the symptoms, not the root of the problem. All of these complexities not only inhibit a leader's ability to find common ground but also inhibit a leader's ability to lead.

Finding common ground is not enough to solve a problem or to move people from one condition to the next. Problems are in search of solution, and people are searching for vision. And just as vital as finding common ground is communicating that vision and rallying people to have a shared vision.

Chapter 2: The Model for Leadership

Unified Thought (U)

The leader in the mirror must share a vision that people can rally behind. It begins with the question, "What vision must I share?" This is not a slogan but a purpose that unifies thought. Inspired by God, Nehemiah set out to fulfill his purpose to rebuild the wall (a way of life) around ancient Jerusalem by reminding them of the Lord's promise, reminding them of their storied history, and reminding them about the results of their prior disobedience. Scripture shares in Proverbs 29:18, "Where there is no revelation, the people cast off restraint."

In other words, if people do not have a sense of purpose, people act on their own accord instead of on one accord with God. Making choices outside of God's purpose was a detriment for them and remains a detriment to us. There were feeble attempts to restore Jerusalem, but overall the people had become accepting of their shameful and sad state. It took someone with an outside perspective and with vision to renew their spirits and rally them around what was a daunting task.

In Nehemiah 2:17-18, Nehemiah said to his people, "You see the bad situation we are in, that Jerusalem is desolate and its gates burned by fire. Come, let us rebuild the wall of Jerusalem so that we will no longer be a reproach." Nehemiah told them how the hand of God had been favorable to him and about the king's words, which were also favorable. Then the people said, "Let us arise and build." Nehemiah clearly included himself in the problem and never blamed anyone for the situation. He helped them confront the reality of the issues at hand. There is an art to influencing and motivating when someone has a list of objections as to why they shouldn't do it. Nehemiah did not err on the side of pleasing people and did not tell them what they wanted, but rather he told them what they needed to hear.

Nehemiah was not an outsider, but anointed by God and equipped by the king with provisions. His provisions included letters to ensure a safe journey and to obtain timber for the city gates, as well as the protection of full army cavalry led by officers. These royal accommodations, authority, and provisions from King Artaxerxes was Nehemiah's resume, which was unique evidence that he was officially supported and, more importantly, that the Lord was acting on his behalf. Sometimes, a leader only has his resume. A typical resume is comprised of facts, figures, and accounts of personal, educational, and professional qualifications and experience. However, to those he leads and serves, a leader's resume must have a story, or else the leader neglects to unify thought with people he leads and serves.

One of the late founders of NFL Films, Ed Sabol, said it best.

"My dad has a great expression," Sabol said when his father's Hall of Fame induction was announced. "'Tell me a fact, and I'll learn. Tell me a truth, and I'll believe. But tell me a story, and it will live in my heart forever.' And now my dad's story will be in Canton, and hopefully that will live forever, too."

Ed was right, and these words are profound. Some people call it a story, and some call it a testimony. I have known and heard some great storytellers. Ed and his father Steve told some great stories. But my all-time favorite storyteller is the Lord Jesus. In Matthew 13:35, Jesus said, "I will open my mouth in parables, I will utter things hidden since the creation of the world." Through His parables, Christ unified us in thought by painting imagery with simple word-pictures to help us understand who God is and what His reign is like, as well as to reach our hearts through our imagination. The leader in the mirror should read His parables, for there are no greater examples of how to present a unified thought, especially when a leader uses God's words genuinely. Nehemiah did this as he reminded the Jewish people of the Lord's promise and unified their thoughts towards wanting to rebuild the wall.

Convincing a starved, desperate, isolated, and broken people to rise up every day and build a wall was a daunting task, especially since no one was getting paid. That had to be some impassioned speech he gave to persuade the Jews to go to work. Notice how he motivates them. Nehemiah clearly states the obvious problem, "You see the bad situation we are in." He called them to action and appealed to their honor, integrity, and self-respect when he said, "Let us rebuild the wall of Jerusalem... and we will no longer be a disgrace." (Nehemiah 2:17)

If it wasn't obvious by resources and entourage, Nehemiah shared his personal testimony of how the Lord had worked things out for him. His journey to Jerusalem gave the people confidence that "the gracious hand of God" would make this effort successful. Covered with God's favor, Nehemiah gave an inspiring speech. The people responded immediately and unanimously with no discussion, "Let us arise and build." Notice the use of "we" and "us" in Nehemiah's words. He was not exempt. He was a

Chapter 2: The Model for Leadership

part of the failures, the tasks at hand, and the future... something greater than themselves. A leader like Nehemiah used godly motivation, not to boast, pacify, manipulate, and exaggerate, but to shake them with the simple truth in love. Leader in mirror, never discount another's passion for the Lord and wanting to be a part of His plans.

Before Nehemiah CUE'd the people, he had to CUE his boss—King Artaxerses. Knowing the king could take Nehemiah's life at any time, and knowing he had stopped the work on the wall before (Ezra 4:21), Nehemiah was fearful, but appeared sad in the presence of the king. Reversing the decrees about Jerusalem would not be easy, but the process had begun before he spoke to the king. Nehemiah moved King Artexerses through private prayer. Leader in the mirror, just pray. Activating the Lord through prayer still works and can soften the hearts of the most difficult people. Pray before you talk to that difficult person or audience. Nehemiah gained trust and discipleship through his body of work as a cupbearer. In the presence of the king, Nehemiah had to avoid some words and use others that the pagan King Artexerses I could relate to. Nehemiah did not risk mentioning "Jerusalem" by name but referred to it in endearing terms; the place of his father's tombs. When you speak to a boss or superior about a difficult subject, place yourself in their shoes. Leader in the mirror, think about how they may receive the news, the vision, or the proposal and use words with which they will identify. Whether the message should spark a sense of urgency or sense of pause, be prepared to stand firm on your words and body of work, but more importantly, stand on prayer to unify people in thought.

Equally Yoked (E)

Have you ever watched two mules plowing a field veer off to one side? Have you ever watched two offensive linemen push a training sled and the sled tips unevenly? Have you ever looked through a set of binoculars and your eyes felt separated? The problem in each of these was that two things should be working together, but something was causing them to be misaligned, unbalanced, not paralleled. In other words, they were not equally yoked. Not being equally yoked causes strain on the system, forces the efforts off course, and makes the task more difficult to accomplish. Nehemiah equally yoked his people. He planned and led a transformation shared by the labor of everyone.

Getting things equally yoked doesn't happen by barging in and trying to force people to "do what you want." Nehemiah did not rush into the execution of his plan, he cautiously and discretely inspected Jerusalem's fortification. He rode around on a donkey, an unassuming animal, to make his assessment. He investigated heavily on the southern side, where Jerusalem experienced the least amount of attacks. He assumed that the north side was completely destroyed; a true consultant understands that he does not have to study everything.

When he defined roles for his people and countrymen, he assigned them to gaps in the wall, ensured they knew what success was, and reinforced the need for sacrifice. He was strategic in assigning the gaps. He assigned Israelites to work and protect the places dearest to their hearts; putting them in locations nearest to their own homes and businesses.

Of course, Nehemiah knew there would be opposition and challenges, but he understood the importance of having the right people around him... as well as who *not* to have. The leader in the mirror has to make tough choices, especially when it comes to who gets involved. He leaned on his brother Hanani and Hananiah the commander of the citadel as trusted captains to help facilitate his purpose of protecting the fifty thousand countrymen. His main opposition was Sanballat the Horonite, the governor of Samaria and Nehemiah's chief political opponent; Tobiah the Ammonite, governor of the Transjordan and another political opponent against the welfare of the Israelites; and Geshem the Arab, Nehemiah's chief religious and business opponent. When they heard about Nehemiah's efforts, they mocked and ridiculed the Israelites, but Tobiah was the most incensed and mocking: "What they are building—if even a fox climbed up on it, he would break down their wall of stones." (Ne 4:3) Tobiah was confident that the Israelites would fail, as they had done previously. They wanted the gaps to stay open, as closing them threatened their political positions. These three and their followers had no sympathy with the generational plight of the Israelites, the project, or the glorification of the Lord in Jerusalem.

Nehemiah knew that he would have to deal with the schemes of these three enemies, but more importantly, he realized that there was no time, no need, or no benefits for diplomacy. There are times when the leader in the mirror must meet challenges head-on and alone. Any sit-

Chapter 2: The Model for Leadership

down with Sanballat, Tobaia, and/or Geshem to share Nehemiah's calling, hear their concerns, or to work out a compromise would have been a mistake. Leaders throughout history often do this when dealing with pertinent issues of the time. Sometimes, as a leader you must circumvent the diplomatic process or else you miss a window to a new season—like "secret" negotiations for shared power in post South African apartheid, executive orders to allow people to stay in the U.S., or lifting punitive sanctions on Cuba. To ensure a new season for his people and to prevent cancers and sabotage, Nehemiah confronted his enemies with courage and took a stand to exclude them from the effort. Nehemiah was clear that this mission was not about them (Me-Now) but about the Lord's glory (God-Glory). Nehemiah did not use the clout of the king's letters, rather he used spiritual clout when he said to them, "The God of heaven will give us success." (Nehemiah 2:20) Leader in the mirror, you must have discernment to know when to work with, confront, and/or oppose people.

Through all of this, Nehemiah did not lean on his own understanding, did not take action against his opponents, but called on God every time. Every time! For he knew the task was God's will and the completion of God's plan that Ezra started with building the temple. This work was not about Nehemiah and those Israelites right there with him, but for the future generations to come. He understood that this restoration project was purposed for a good future. The future was his purpose. This effort was more than building a wall, it was about closing the gaps. He spent 52 days closing gaps on the wall, and in doing so, closed gaps between history and hearts of the people, rich and poor, hypocrisy and truth, and his own grief and joy.

Nehemiah led a starved, doubtful, desperate, disobedient, isolated, people by getting them onCUE with God's will, onCUE with the calling on his life, and onCUE with purpose. Nehemiah rejected help from foes as well as non-foes. I can understand not accepting help from foes, but initially found it peculiar that he rejected help from non-foes. Upon further study, I realized that the reason he said "no" to their help was that those non-foes could not get onCUE. They may have been friendly, but he had to put some of those non-foes in the same category as foes. Why? Nehemiah shared reason when he answered initially the ridicule of Sanballat, Tobiah, and Geshem in Nehemiah chapter 2 verse 20: "...but as for you, you have no share in Jerusalem or any claim or historic right to it." Although non-foes shared the vision or the unified thought, non-foes did not meet the first huddle of having common ground. They had no share in Jerusalem, no historic right, and no claim in its future. Why was this important? Nehemiah knew that times would get tough for his people and did not need others, who did not have a right to Jerusalem, to potentially quit on him during tough times. If the non-foes did not quit, they could negatively impact morale and become a cancer, destroying from within. They didn't have a stake in the future or skin in the game. We have all met people who do not have the staying-power when times get tough. We know people in our midst who are disruptive and never have anything good to say. It is vital for the leader in the mirror to be wise enough to prevent these cancers and bold enough to get rid of them. If not, the gap widens and puts future generations at risk.

The leader in the mirror must understand the tension and challenge to discover how to be on one accord with God. Being on CUE with the Lord is being in perfect harmony with Him. I once had a prominent musician on our radio show. From a long line of servant leaders, he is an accomplished teacher and lover of music. He shared that tension in music harmony is a good thing. More tension builds the perfect harmony. There is plenty of tension building in our society, impeding our ability to focus on the future. However, at the same time, mounting tension allows for greater glory to God to be shown. God wants to use us, but we have to be willing. Another one of God's transformational leaders perhaps said it best. In his 1994 inauguration speech, Nelson Mandela quoted from Marianne Williamsons' *Course of Miracles*:

> "Our deepest fear is not that we are inadequate. Our deepest fear is that we are powerful beyond measure. It is our light, not our darkness that most frightens us. We ask ourselves, Who am I to be brilliant, gorgeous, talented, fabulous? Actually, who are you not to be? You are a child of God. Your playing small does not serve the world. There is nothing enlightened about shrinking so that other people won't feel insecure around you. We are all meant to shine, as children do. We were born to make manifest the glory of God that is within us. It's not just in some of us; it's in everyone.

Chapter 2: The Model for Leadership

And as we let our own light shine, we unconsciously give other people permission to do the same. As we are liberated from our own fear, our presence automatically liberates others."

Then Mandela went on to say, "Last evening, we were gathered in the church basement speaking together about common values. A young child asked, 'What was the scariest moment that you faced when you were homeless? What disturbed you more than at any time when you were on the streets?' Before I answer this precise and articulate question we must remind ourselves that all of us are special even when we refuse to accept this mantle. All life is a precious, irreplaceable gift. We are all angels given to all the world to sing in perfect harmony."

Mandela expressed that we all have a purpose and must take up our mantle to make a difference and not waste this precious life that God has given us. We are each different with a different purpose on different tones. But when we line up the different tones, while working within our purpose, our rhythm is in sync and in one accord. We are on CUE in perfect harmony if and only if we are on accord with the Lord.

We need leaders at the fabric of society taking up the mantle, making a difference. What do I mean by fabric of society? My father-in-law Dr. Joseph C. Pentecoste, a former university professor and consultant for many Chicago area urban projects, revealed it to me. I never met him, for he passed away before I met my Tai (my wife). To understand the man who had influenced my future wife, I watched some of his taped lectures. Dr. Pentecoste believed that all things in our society can be grouped into one of four facets: politics, economics, social matters, and education. He stressed the importance of understanding the interconnection, interdependence, and interrelations of these four facets. In one of his lectures, he said, "We mustn't change one (facet) without assessing the affects on the others!" Changes in one impacts the others, and it can be a matter of degrees to which they are impacted. He went on to say, "In order for a society to truly flourish, these facets must be balanced."

The facets are like pillars; pillars which stand side-by-side to support and uphold society. Although they are side-by-side, politics dictates the terms and the make-up of the other three. Politics are the first filter in the decision-making of a society. Political correctness rules the day in the news, government, businesses, churches, little league fields, home, and schools.

Following that, the social pillar seems to carry more weight than the others. When I first heard Dr. Pentecoste speak of the pull that the social facet has, I initially questioned it. But I have learned through experience that he was right. He said, "He who controls the minds and hearts, controls society." That is being proved out now as well as it has been in the past.

I term these four facets / pillars as the Societal Ecosystem©. Today, our ecosystem is warped and out of balance. I think this is largely because of the social and political pillars. Why? Remember from chapter 1, the "I" in the D.E.V.I.L. that plagues our culture and is tearing the fabric is **irreverence** to God's presence, power, love, wrath, and dominion. Without the proper anchor, one is tossed by any new phenomena the Me-Now culture creates. I'm not sure if Dr. Penteoste had a solution in mind, but I believe that it is time for the leader in the mirror to take his place in bringing balance back to our Societal Ecosystem.

Societal Ecosystem©

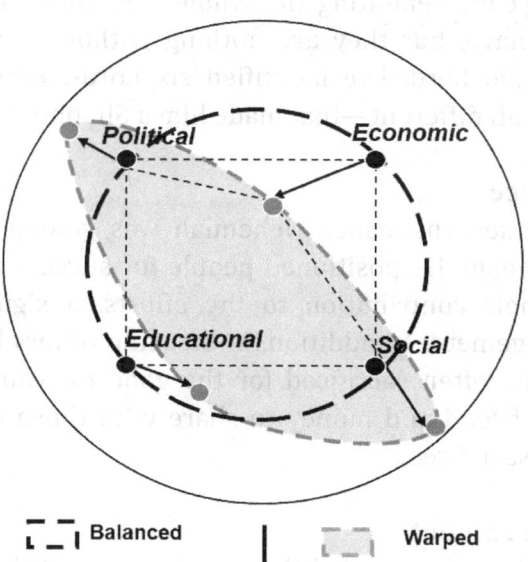

There are stark parallels in the events in the Book of Nehemiah to my time in St. Louis and to today. We are warned against this imbalance

Chapter 2: The Model for Leadership

in Scripture. Ephesians 4:14-16 reads: "We will no longer be infants, tossed back and forth by the waves, and blown here and there by every wind of teaching and by the cunning and craftiness of people in their deceitful scheming. Instead, speaking the truth in love, we will grow to become in every respect the mature body of him who is the head, that is, Christ. From him the whole body, joined and held together by every supporting ligament, grows and builds itself up in love, as each part does its work."

The social and political pillars create the doctrine that is tossing our children about. How do we return to a calm balance? Who is the model? More importantly, what are the qualities to emulate?

Seldom are there models to emulate as Nehemiah, who truly defined transformational leadership. He was an expert craftsman, worked as cupbearer for King Artaxerses I, and most importantly, had a personal brand that was sustained by faith, with God as his point of reverence. He empowered, with purpose and direction, a broken people from a discourse of disgrace, shame, and desperation in rebuilding ancient Jerusalem's walls and way of life. This example may lead to debate among some religions, but Nehemiah was a true change agent who broke cycles, benefiting the whole. Yes, there are many qualities that leaders have, but they are nothing without being rooted in and anointed by the Lord. I've identified six Lord-anointed qualities that made Nehemiah different—that made him a Shepherd.

1. Service

Truly a servant leader, Nehemiah was guided by service rather than opportunism. He positioned people for success and greatness and celebrated their contribution to the efforts, a signature element of change management. In addition, influencing others by his love of God and people, he often sacrificed for the good of whole by forgoing his entitlement of food and money to share with those that were in more need. This is sacrifice.

2. Discernment

Political opposition and the pure enemies of the rebuilding never rested. Nehemiah was equipped with discernment that was rooted in the Lord. He handled and made right decisions regarding lies and deceit that enemies portrayed, without having the benefits of all the facts. Often even-tempered, Nehemiah knew whether to be indignant or voiceless when dealing with threats. How to be wise with limited wisdom? The Lord knows what we do not.

3. Persistence

Nehemiah knew that he only needed to be as persistent as his foes and challenges, and not any more. This lesson is crucial when handling issues. He met them at every challenge, but did not linger on the "battlefield" waiting to demonstrate how tough he was.

4. Integrity

Given that he was the king's cupbearer, he had to have been trustworthy with unquestionable integrity. His body of work may or may not have warranted such trust from others, but Nehemiah was reinforced with God-molded integrity. Your integrity benchmark must be to stay aligned with what God says.

5. Philosophy

Not constrained by his own philosophy, he was guided strictly by God's calling and purpose. He focused on and reinforced change for the good of God's glory and united people in love and service for God's purpose, not his own. If your philosophy is God's philosophy, it will be anointed.

6. Gamesmanship

He held God as his only point of reverence or first filter in making decisions. Nehemiah was not a political animal, but he was not naive to think politics wasn't a factor. As such, he found common ground, and attracted a diverse set of views, experiences, and backgrounds. He got them on one accord. His game was on.

These qualities, anointed by God, guided him as he managed challenges that directly and indirectly affected him. With God's favor, Nehemiah was guided by service, rather than opportunism. He was equipped with discernment, particularly when dealing with foes and challenges. And, he was blessed with unquestionable integrity. All of this frames his philosophy and gamesmanship in dealing with the problems and politics of the day. Meeting his Divine appointment and receiving anointment allowed Nehemiah's leadership to illuminate and garner trust and discipleship. He was accused of accepting kick-backs in exchange of favors; he battled the practice of mortgaging lifetime human labor for meat and other basic essentials; and he secured the economics (fish and spice trades) as the first step in nation-building before solving social, political, and educational issues. Yet, Nehemiah led the exiles in rebuilding the walls of Jerusalem while navigating them through times of doubt and despair that resemble our modern-day issues and challenges in the world. God's favor garnered foundational trust and discipleship that kept the exiles on CUE, even in times of doubt and despair. Few experience such presence, but the good news is that we can seek it now.

If the leader in the mirror has these anointed qualities, he can transform challenges that warp and tear at the fabric of our society, which parallels those in ancient Jerusalem. The world has had various philosophies with differing notions of truth, values, and virtues by which one should live. CUE Leadership is not about values to live by but values to die by. When we serve God in our leadership, we die to ourselves. The Bible tells us in Luke 17:33 that "Whoever seeks to keep his life will lose it; and whoever loses his life will preserve it."

The question for the leader in the mirror is: "Are you willing to die for it?" It is in serving God that you meet the Me-Now culture at the gaps and begin to save our uncommitted, desperate, starved, isolated, shamed, I.D.L.E. generation. It is in serving God that the leader in the mirror will become truly transformational.

Chapter 3:
DYSFUNCTIONAL LEADERSHIP

CUE LEADERSHIP MATRIX©

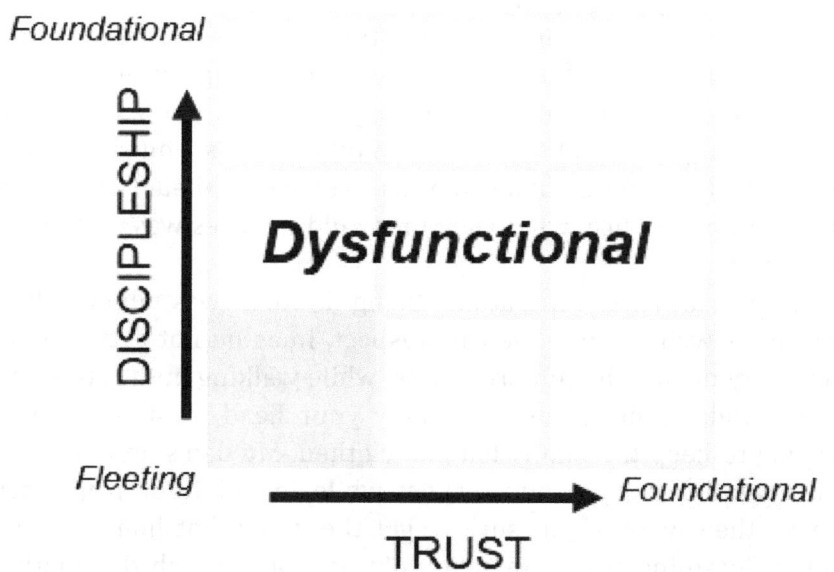

"Ya be whatcha see."
—Hugh Mack Peagler, Sr.

    I love watching reruns of *The Cosby Show* and I love the fact that my girls love to watch them, too. It reminds me of watching *Bonanza* with Dad as a child and even later as an adult. Dad used to say that I reminded him of Little Joe—trying to find my way. Just like Mr. Cartwright had done for his generation, Dr. Heathcliff Huxtable inspired my generation by showing us something different by setting expectations for his kids. He made it a normal thing to expect effort, to expect truth, to expect great careers, to expect a college degree, to expect results, and to expect a future. It is amazing what having

Chapter 3: Dysfunctional Leadership

expectations will do and how television, music, and culture can shape us. I was shaped by many things—my parents, sports, our community, church, and the world. When I look back, especially when looking at old pictures from college and high school, a few things strike me. In my poses, I was either trying to look suave or fresh for the ladies (in my clothes, haircut, waves, sunglasses), showing my toughness (through my facial expression, ripped muscles, or clenched fists), or trying to draw attention to my "gifts" (my manhood).

We learned to present ourselves this way, which has been passed down through the generations. Growing up during my generation in "L.A." (Lower Alabama), either you played sports, got your lesson in school, chased girls, or all the above. In other words, you strove to be a young buck. If you were not any of those, you were labeled as less than a man, or a punk. Hence, what I see in my old pictures was myself trying to be that "buck."

In my father's generation, being a man was about physical posturing as well as about getting respect. Imagine not getting respect from society during the Jim Crow time, while walking in the street, fresh in your Sunday's best, having to bow your head in submission, and struggling to keep the family fed and clothed. My dad's and his father's generations did not get due respect while in public or from society. However, they were "d__n" sure to get the respect at home, even if it meant maintaining complete strict, physical, and tough domination of things they *could* control. No matter what generation, there is a truth that we must confront. If we aren't careful, the physical might not just shape us; it might define us.

With that in mind, I have a good friend who has an interesting theory on the impacts of black men being sold on slave auction generations ago. Given two points:

1. Being defined in the physical sense (slave auctions wanted the "bucks"), and
2. Being separated from their families,

led to a deterioration in men learning what it meant to be the spiritual leader of the household. The family matriarchs were forced to hold the family together and be the spiritual leaders; taking kids to church, reading the Bible, providing hope, etc. Of course, this does not apply to every father today, but it is worthwhile to consider how the leader in the mirror defines him/herself. Primarily physical or primarily spiritual? It is a tough question, but a legitimate one we must ask.

This was painfully true with many men in our family, especially my maternal grandfather, Hugh Mack Peagler, Sr. He had many legendary one-liners and sayings that were simple but filled with wisdom. He was my idol for a long time.

I thought my grandpops was the greatest storyteller who ever lived. He had this magnetic personality that made people want to be around him. When I talked to him, he made me feel like I was the only person that mattered at that time. He had a way of convincing us to do something that we did not want to do. Afterwards, we felt great about it. Grandpops stressed values of "keeping your word" and "leaving someone better than you found them." Words from his mouth were like honey dripping off his lips. He had a silver tongue… the gift of gab.

One of his sayings that sticks with me is: "Ya be whatcha see, unless ya have a 'bellious spirit." What he meant was that if I saw "good" in life, I would be "good" in life, but if I had a rebellious spirit, I would be "bad." He meant it conversely as well. If I saw "bad" in life, I would be "bad" in life, but if I had a rebellious spirit against what I saw, then I would be "good." There remains much validity and painful wisdom in those words. He was a lifelong sharecropper with little education and under the demented control of a plantation landowner. He escaped through chasing woman and drinking hard. He saw himself as a buck and had a way with women. He did not always do right by my grandmother, Ma Eva. He shared stories and escapades with my brother Jody and me of his stepping out on Ma Eva. At the time we weren't sure why he shared those details and I'm not sure why we were not ticked off at him. But he would always finish our talks by saying: "I am what I am." He would often tell us that he was not perfect.

My questions as to why he would share such things were answered on his last day on this earth. He left me with words of honey and used that silver tongue to deposit words of wisdom that I carry with me today. Grandpops had been suffering in last few months of life. He was in and out between the hospital, nursing home, and his home. It was a tough time for our family, but he was never alone. Among my Aunt Doris, my mother, Uncle Hugh Jr., and the rest of the family, we were

Chapter 3: Dysfunctional Leadership

always there or nearby. During his last few weeks, he was in the hospital, and his breathing had noticeably worsened. On my last day of high school, I stopped by after school, excited about finishing, looking forward to summer, anxious for college, and excited about the parties!

When I arrived in his room, he was sitting up in bed with the oxygen mask on, but with a spark in his eye. I knew that he was excited to see me. He asked Mom to let me have her chair next to his bed. Then, he did something strange. He asked Mom and Aunt Doris to leave the room because he wanted to talk to me. Mom and Aunt Doris looked at each other with confusion and did what he asked.

Once they closed the door, Grandpops asked me to open a "Pipsy Cola" (Pepsi) and share it with him. I added ice to two small styrofoam cups, opened the Pepsi, and poured one cup. Grandpops said, "No, give me the can." I guess he wanted to feel normal and did not want to sip from a hospital straw. He asked me to sit down. He pulled off the oxygen mask and placed it at his chin, then he began.

"Ready for yo' speech?" he asked, referring to my speech as class president.

I said, "Yes, sir."

"Well, you make us proud. Continua' to do what ya' doing. I still can't believe a child of mine was on T.V. like you was." Grandpops was referring to my interview and honor as a finalist for the WAKA-Church's Chicken Scholar Athlete of the Year and Bryant-Jordan Award. The WAKA-Church's Chicken Award was a regional award, but the Bryant-Jordan Award was named for the late great coaches Paul "Bear" Bryant of University of Alabama and Ralph "Shug" Jordan of Auburn University. The Bryant-Jordan Award recipient was selected from the top student-athletes in the entire state. Although I did not win, I was one the six finalists. My granddaddy was proud of that, and proud that I'd be heading off to college on a football scholarship. He went on to say, "Do whatcha momma say and do good. You are our hope."

My heart raced because this was sounding like a goodbye. Grandpops shifted to an unexpected subject as he said, "When you get married, don't do your wife like I did Honey," (what he called Ma Eva) "cause you won't find a woman like her. When you get married, put the Lawd first, maker her yo' best friend, and keep yo' family and friends out yo' business."

I was confused why he was telling his 17 year old grandson about marriage. I was off to college on a football scholarship, where I heard the ratio for girls to boys was 5 to 1. Marriage was not on my radar. So, I interrupted and said, "Pops, I am not thinking about getting married."

He quickly snapped back, "Hush up boy. Two ears, one mouth." So, I hushed up. He took another deep breath of oxygen and went on to say, "Thangs will get tuff. If ya ev'r thank it is time to leave, split-up, go yo' separate ways, or divorce, ask yo'self: if you knew that that day was her last on God's earth, how would you treat her? Ask yo'self that whenever that time comes." Wow, he had my attention with a nugget that I have shared with so many throughout my life. Then he ended with something more unexpected and said, "And last thang. Make my name great!"

All of these words, especially his last words, "Make my name great," stuck with me. After he spoke, we just looked at each other, and I wanted to ask him what he meant. But I remembered, "two ears and one mouth." I looked in silence into his greyed eyes. Then Pops broke the moment by saying, "Now give yo' granddaddy a hug and get out of here. Go have some fun! I'd be alright."

He put his oxygen mask back on, and I left. After a night full of fun, I went home rather than to go back by the hospital. After Class Night ceremonies, Mom left to cover her shift at the hospital. Around 2 A.M., a car driving down our dirt road woke me. It sounded like Uncle Hugh's truck. It was, and I heard the door open and Mom tell Uncle Hugh, "Junior, I will see you in the morning."

I knew then that Granddaddy had died. I heard Dad meet Mom at the door and greet her saying, "Sorry. He is in better place. Are you OK?"

They talked for a second, and then she made her way down the hall to me and Jody. She did not have to say it, but she said it anyway, "Dad's gone. You know he loved y'all. He didn't suffer. He went in peace." Later, I learned that in his final moments, the rough breathing stopped, and he breathed normally until he took his final breath. In that season of my life, I felt like a part of me died with him. I carried an anger in me for a long time after that. He was more than a grandfather, for he was truly a best friend and one with a dying wish.

I struggled with the meaning of his dying wish for me. He spoke life into my life. He wanted me to be an instrument to wash away his legacy of being the willing "buck." When people heard his name, they

Chapter 3: Dysfunctional Leadership

would not respond as a gentlemen responded to his name about 8-10 years prior. We never talked about the incident, but it had to have been on his mind...

I had spent the weekend with a friend, Chris Carter, at his home in Braggs Hill. Braggs Hill is small community in Forest Home. Church was over, and everyone was fellowshipping on the church grounds. When Chris' grandmother introduced me to people from their church, she did it in the traditional way; not by my full name, Eric Powell. Rather she introduced me first as "a Powell" and then as "Tommie and Sarah Powell's son." My first name was never said. One of the ladies in crowd restated, "Sarah Powell. Are you talking about Sarah Peagler, Miss Eva's and Hugh Mack's girl?"

Chris' grandmother said, "Yes Ma'am. That's her."

Then a man standing nearby said in a joking, but informed, way to the other men in the crowd, "Hugh Mack's grandson? Booooy, y'all better grab your wives and hide'em."

What did he mean by that? I'd wondered.

I never forgot those words. And then low and behold... A few minutes later, I see Granddaddy. At church? Sitting by a lady? He never went to church with Ma Eva or with us until years later, but he was at church in Braggs Hill? That thought lasted a millisecond as I ran to him. We talked and hugged on each other, and then I said goodbye because it was time to go. As I hugged him, he told me to reach in his pocket and get the three "candy fitty cents" pieces (Kennedy fifty cent). He never said not mention that I saw him, but as I look back, the fifty-cent pieces said it, and his eyes said it.

Sitting me down and sharing a Pepsi could have been his way of bringing that moment back in my mind. He wanted me to be a catalyst in breaking a cycle in our family of which God was not pleased. Pops knew that one of the most important, most vital decisions that I would make in life would be who I chose as my bride; the woman with whom I would spend the rest of my life. He had told me in confidence that he wished that my Uncle Hugh, who recently had divorced, would reunite with his wife before Grandpops passed. Grandpops felt that he had failed Uncle Hugh, and especially did not deserve having his loving Honey and family around him in his last days, after all he had done. He wanted me to break the cycle and did not want my marriage marred to infidelity because it would lead only to pain and strife. I guess I was his second chance. I chose well for a variety of reasons. Yes, I made a promise to my grandfather; and I made a wholehearted promise to Tai. But most importantly, Tai and I made a covenant with the Lord. We pray that the Lord continues to be glorified through our marriage.

Why this story? Although I spoke mostly of my grandfather, this really is a story of a faithful, forgiving, loving, God-fearing woman. My grandmother, Ma Eva; who believed in "till death do us part" and the story of redemption and God's grace in action with my granddaddy. Grandpops had a rebellious spirit, yet he walked the redemption road back to Christ. The Lord gave him peace and the power of the Holy Spirit. His breakthrough moment was at our Christmas dinner in 1990 at my Aunt Doris' home. She was the main caretaker of Ma Eva and Granddaddy. That Christmas, Granddaddy led us in the most unexpected prayer. Seldom in my life have I (we) heard a more thunderous prayer. His task was to bless the food, but he brought the Lord's spirit into that dining room like I had never felt or heard before. It is difficult to describe how he wrapped pain, sorrow, joy, love, redemption, humbleness, thunder, power, and uplifting into his words, building to a true place of redemption. He pleaded for forgiveness, thanked the Lord for His grace, thanked the Lord for Honey, who he said he never deserved, and pleaded with Jesus to hear his voice that had not praised His name like this before. Granddaddy told that Lord that he knew that he was at the end of his "journey," but he wanted Him to cover and bless his family.

Granddaddy could not read well. He told me that the only thing he could write was his name that Ma Eva taught him to draw, not write. So these words obviously came from his marrow, and there was not a dry eye in the room—from kids to adults. There was power in Jesus' name. That day marked the day where he became new. I can't describe it any better. He went to church soon after that and wanted to hear my Aunt Leola, Mom's youngest sister, sing his favorite song, "He'll Understand and Say, 'Well Done.'"

His dying wish, his Christmas prayer, and his favorite song were redemption for that farm boy who was a sharecropper all of his life. He and Ma Eva worked the land and raised crops, animals, and family on a promise of making money for the Poole Family, the landowners. The

Chapter 3: Dysfunctional Leadership

more children they had, the better the harvest would be.

To survive while working the land, our family and other families would trade at the local store for basic essentials. If we had cash to pay, we paid it. But most of the time, they paid on store credit. This credit was not based on a FICO score but rather:
- on Granddaddy's word—his integrity, and
- on who spoke for or vouched for him, his name, and his identity.

Having a great harvest and keeping both his integrity and identity intact ware critical in paying off store credit and maintaining it for the next season as well as for the next generation. If the harvest, integrity, or identity waned, the resulting work and spending created mounds of debt that were almost impossible to pay. The health and welfare of his children were tied to all three. He was a hard worker, but one of the three waned constantly outside of his work. His identity became compromised through his infidelity, but when the harvest did not come in, he did what he had to in order to maintain his "buck" status—even if that meant taking all of the kids' earnings from the harvest or taking from the Pooles without them knowing. Good or bad, he did it. And he suffered or enjoyed the consequences. But for God, he was saved.

Our struggles were not different from those who lived on that plantation or who were challenged to get basic essentials. As Ecclesiates shares, "there is nothing new under the sun," and this is true even with the practice of exchanging human labor for meat and other basic essentials. This happened in generations before me, and it is happening now. It happened in Nehemiah's time in the form of usury. In Nehemiah chapter 5, we read of this struggle and shared suffering of the Isrealites caused by piles of illegitimate debt. They had no food and large mortgages, they borrowed money to pay taxes, and they were enslaved to debtholders. Nehemiah had to act. He had to get all the people—debtors and debtholders—to act and behave differently, hence creating a new legacy. Nehemiah focused on where he could make the most change in terms of the people's behavior and went to the root of the problem. He confronted them boldly and called them out on usury.

The Isrealites had already bought as many of their own people back from the Gentiles as they could. But now, the nobles were selling them back with all of the new illegitimate debt. Nehemiah shamed them and called on them to stop this practice and forgive the debt. The nobles agreed. However, Nehemiah did not stop there. He summoned the priest and got them to take an oath in the presence of Almighty God. In this way, he said that God will "shake out" the houses and possessions for who does not keep this promise. Nehemiah went on to say, "So may such a man be shaken out and emptied!" He reminded them of the promise and their historic right to Jerusalem and their need to sacrifice for the future.

Granddaddy's words were about the future and about a promise. When he asked everyone to leave the hospital room except for me, he knew there were words he needed to impart to me before he left the earth. Those words and his command to make his name great molded my future actions. In that last conversation, he became more than a grandfather; he was a mentor, a leader, my best friend.

It wasn't a fancy education that drove Granddaddy to have that wisdom; it was the education from having Christ in his life that guided his words. They've come back to me often and one example occurred around Easter 2013. I went to court with my nephew, who had placed himself in some trouble. It was a trying time for him and a trying time for all of our family, because my dad had passed away the prior weekend. As I sat in the court, I observed youth after youth go before the judge. I recognized some of them, or at least recognized some of their features and could make an educated guess who they were related to. Each of them put on their best face and were wearing their best club outfit. Then, the time came for my nephew to go before the judge. The judge seemed less stoic, or less stern, with him. Once their discussion was done, the judge called my nephew close and spoke to him. Then he shook my nephew's hand. The judge had not done that with anyone else. My nephew was in quite a different mood as we left the courtroom. I asked what the judge said to him when he called him close. The judge told him that he would help as much as he could and wanted my nephew to come back to him if my nephew had any problems.

I asked, "Why did the judge shake your hand?"

My nephew replied, "The judge told me that he was sorry to

Chapter 3: Dysfunctional Leadership

hear about Granddaddy. That's a good sign, huh?"

I sharply told him, "Don't be mistaken, and don't fool yourself. The judge was not shaking your hand. He was shaking your granddaddy's hand, his father's hand, and Granddaddy Hugh Mack's hand, not yours. You see, they helped to raise that judge on their plantation, and they, along with a whole host of folks in the family, have built up capital with him and have deposited money (service) in the bank with his family."

I speak from experience. Spending that capital without making a deposit creates a debt that you cannot pay. What my nephew was going through was exactly what Granddaddy wanted to change for us. My nephew was a dysfunctional leader with a rebellious streak. He had two ears and three mouths. He was "being what he was seeing."

The nobles in the time of Nehemiah were not unlike a younger version of Granddaddy, my nephew, or me. They were dysfunctional leaders—transparent, shallow, and burdened by heavy gamesmanship and philosophy. They were leading a generation on a road of failure and were guided by inflexible principles that were focused on self. Not until the Lord sent a catalyst for transformation via pain and brokenness through Nehemiah's leadership did these dysfunctional leaders confront reality. They were being what they were seeing, not realizing that the integrity and identity of the future generation was at stake. Nehemiah made them see that the *future* was their purpose, just as Granddaddy wanted his hard work and his contribution to his family and to society to be "great."

The good news is that God's anointing can raise the most dysfunctional person to be transformational. The Lord can lift the self-imposed weights and build foundational discipleship and trust just as He did with Granddaddy and with the nobles; and as He will do with my nephew and his children. Any leader in the mirror, even the dysfunctional ones with a rebellious streak, can be transformed. Our heavenly Father has placed a promise and the legacy of His name on Jesus... make His name great!

Although my transformation is in progress, I too was dysfunctional like Granddaddy, like my nephew, like the plantation owner, even like Jim Crow. I was a walking oxymoron. I was what I saw and had a rebellious spirit. Personally, that makes for a hardened heart; self-absorbed, fearful of failure, angry but smart, talented, gifted with endless promise. I was caught between it all and was always trying to prove something, changing and adapting like a chameleon, and trying to be something that I was not. I went from mimicking Optimus Prime to Michael Jackson to Prince to Malcolm X to Dewayne Wayne (from the Cosby series *A Different World*). I even had the prescription flip-up eyeglasses. The oxymoron manifested in my nicknames or what people accused me of over the years—Mighty Mouse, Smart Jock, Little Giant, or Black Republican.

My dad's friend, Mr. Bay Williams, called me "Mighty Mouse" as child. "You are small but you play tall," he rhymed. I am not sure if I ever "saved the day" like Mighty Mouse did on the cartoon. The confidence in my ability to "play tall" never wavered until a sobering and piercing comment was made during our sports awards banquet in the spring of my 11th grade year. A high school football booster called me the "Smart Jock" in one second and gave me a backhand compliment in the next second. He said, "I am glad that you are smart because you will never play college football like your brothers. You are just too small."

How could he think that? He saw that I was holding the MVP trophy at one the top football powerhouses in the state. Why would he deflate me like that? You would think that the comments would have fueled me to prove him wrong, but instead, he wounded me that night. For the first time, I thought about my size in terms of sports. For the first time, I went home and measured myself. For the first time, the fear of failure (not living up to expectations set by my two legendary brothers) consumed the urge to prove the football booster wrong. To hedge failure, I decided to get out front of the story... I calculated that if I told the world that I did not want to play, it wouldn't see me as a failure as compared to Jody and Tom. I began to say that I was not going to play sports in college and that I was going to focus on academics. It was plausible. The campaign went so well that my coaches began to tell college recruiters the story. A coach

Chapter 3: Dysfunctional Leadership

from Southern Mississippi just shook his head in frustration because he had come all that way for nothing. The coach at Samford University and who came from a well-known coaching family wanted to check me for a fever. Coach after coach came and left with the impression that I was not like my brothers. If the coaches' visits were not evidence enough that the football booster was wrong and that I needed to stop the charade, the next two things were. My high school teammate and future college teammate, Paul Jones, tracked me down and said, "I heard that you were not taking your visits. You are so smart to where you're stupid!" Now, that was an oxymoron. He went on to say, "If you are not going to play, that is OK, but at least take the visits. We are taking about cooooollege with college girrrrrrrls at coooolllllegge parrrrtiiees!" He said that last part slowly so his message would sink in. He was right. My charade and I were stupid because I *wanted* to play. It was all that I dreamed of doing. I had completely forgotten about watching Auburn great "Little Train" Lionel James in the same backfield with Bo Jackson. That next week, the effects of my campaign worked so well to where it hurt. One of my coaches told me that a coach from Yale had come by, but he told him that I did not want to play in college. Yale? Ouch! You may ask yourself, "Why didn't coaches try a little harder?" Why would they? Why would they recruit a player who said he does not want to play?

My scheme was purely dysfunctional. I read too much of someone else's press and made my over-calculation the result instead of proving the booster wrong. I saw him later after we won the national championship and casually flashed my ring in his face while buying something at his country store. Yes, it was a little arrogant of me, but by that time, I had been reading my own press. I did not realize that I was still doing dysfunctional things on a downward spiral, and my ride was my intelligence, football, and W.W.N.

Football had become my god, and the Lord knew it. I took pride in the smart jock utility, especially after being named the small college player of the week in *Sports Illustrated*. It was the October 1992 issue with George Brett on the front for reaching the 3,000 hit milestone. After Chuck and Cory went down from injuries, I had stopped my rotation as runningback and played quarterback. I was listed as third string quarterback to allow us to carry an extra linebacker, but who knew I would have to play it? I ran the double option all day (as I had in high school) and led our team to victory with 100+ yards rushing, 2 touchdowns, and 2-2 pass completions. It was awesome. But my teammate should have never shown me that article as we were on the way to play in Mississippi. I was listed as the number one quarterback. My head was big enough as it was, but that just proved how good I thought I was. The Lord served me up some humble pie because that next game was the worst I have ever played. I could not remember a call, an assignment, or a read. I left my playbook and intelligence back at the rest stop before I read that article. I got benched from quarterback and was not put into the runningback rotation. It was a bad day and my head was not in the game.

But I really left my intelligence on the field as we neared the playoffs. Before the end of the first half of a game, I caught a pitch during an option play, turned the corner, and cut back into the field. I did not see the safety coming and did not have time to make myself smaller (less surface area to hit). He hit me hard. What a lick! As I was falling backwards, I said to myself that I was going to get up first and quick to show the safety that the hit was nothing... I was not going to give him the satisfaction even though my bell was rung. As soon as my back hit the ground, I benchpressed him off of me and jumped up. But my head was throbbing and the stadium seem to spin around me. A little dazed, I just followed the red jerseys back to the huddle. Chuck asked me if I was alright. I told him that lick was nothing. So Chuck ran the next play and then the next, and then the half was over. Halftime helped me get my head clear. I never told anyone how dazed I was. I played the rest of the game. Coach David Sikes (our running back coach) took the starters out (I was starting again after the disastrous start earlier in the year). After being on the sideline for a while, the staduim began to spin. I called a trainer, who then went to get our head trainer, the ageless Jim Skidmore.

Chapter 3: Dysfunctional Leadership

Coach Skid came over, looked at me, and asked, "Was the hit before the half? I nodded, "Yes." He said that he almost pulled me, but he saw me pop up as I ususally do when I get tackled. I told him I couldn't give the safety the satisfaction that he hurt me because he had been talking trash all day. As he was checking me out, Coach Skid called me a "hard-headed dumb ***" for not telling him and told the staff trainer to take me to the locker room.

Sure enough, I had a grade 1 concussion. Later that night at a victory party, I asked Jason, my roommate, to drive me back to the dorm. The pain had worsened. Morning came. I felt like I had been hit by a brick. I had to go to the training room to see Coach Skid. Jason got up and asked me if I was OK. I told him that I was and left our dorm room. I walked down the hall on the red carpet, but when I reached the stairway I realized something. I felt the cold vinyl under my feet and realized that I forgot to put my shoes on... *uh oh...* I went back to the room. Jason got more concerned when I told him that I forgot my shoes. He asked if I wanted him to drive me over. I told him again that I was OK. Back down the stairs I went, and then into the lobby to go out the door. Through the shades on the window, I could tell that it was a sunny day. However, as soon as I opened the door, the sun stunned me. I acted like Dracula as I tried to block the sun because it was too bright. I began to get really worried and almost went to get Jason. As soon as I turned back to take his offer of a ride, Jason was walking in the lobby. Not to show weakness, I told him that I was good to go. My eyes adjusted a little, and I walked the 100+ yard trek to the training room with my eyes half shut.

I was nauseous as I entered the training room, and everyone looked at me similar to Jason's puzzled look. Coach Skid looked over his glasses, and concern covered his face. He gave me a sobriety test. I followed his pen back and forth. Then he asked me to stretch my arms, close my eyes, and touch my nose. I closed my eyes, and when I opened them, I was looking up at one of the staff trainers who caught me before I hit the floor. I did not realize that I had fallen. This was serious. I heard Coach Skid instruct someone to call Dr. Goodlett to tell him the situation and ask him what hospital we should meet him at, to call Coach Burgess and tell him that he was taking Eric Powell to the hospital, and to get the number for Mr. & Mrs. Powell and get them on the phone. I tried to convince Coach that I was fine. He ignored me. Although this grading scale has been eliminated in today's concussion testing, my concussion went from grade 1 to almost a grade 6.

I spent from Sunday to Tuesday in the hospital. It was a trying, scary time. I could not stay awake, but nurses woke me up every hour on the hour from my sleep, asking me simple questions like who wrote the Gettysburg Address, what was my name, or what was my mother's name? Sadly, it took me a while to remember Mom's face. I panicked many times. Once I was released, I had to stay inside because I could not bear to be in the sunlight. I missed three weeks of classes. Knowing what we know now, I probably would not have played again. Besides the countless number of MRIs, I went through a rigorous battery of testing to get back on the field. The testing was a brutal set of drills, sprints, and exercises. The goal was to make it through the entire test standing and make it through with a clear head. I failed miserably the first time. I did not complete the set of drills and missed another game. Playoffs were approaching, and I was not about to miss another run to the "show" since we lost the championship game the prior year. The second test was just as brutal. I completed the drills, but my head was throbbing. The stadium was swimming, but I lied and said that my head was clear. Yes, I lied. If I had been truthful about my condition I probably would not have played again.

Although we won the National Championship that year, I lost something that I held dear... my ability to absorb and comprehend information. I lost the intelligence that I savored, took pride in, and flaunted arrogantly. Before that moment, I never really had to study hard. I could hear it, see it, and work it. All subjects came easy to me. After that concussion, I began to make bad grades and did not know why. I could not grasp subject matter in an instant, process it, and play it back like I used to. Studying harder did not work. As a math major, I had to find another way. I had to teach myself how to study

Chapter 3: Dysfunctional Leadership

all over again.

God had called me long before this, but I had taken my eyes off Him and made other worldly things my god. Just like the game after the *Sports Illustrated* article, my head was not in the game—God's game. Smart jock (my intelligence and football) had become my god. I was failing in schooling and in football, especially after we moved up to Division 1-AA. I did not know why. It fueled more anger in me, but it also fueled shame and a deep depression. Worse than that, I was having an identity crisis, lacked a sense of purpose and direction, and did not have the ability to cope with failure. I had become less what the Birmingham Herald declared as the "Little Giant" and was just little. A dysfunctional mixture of anger, shame, depression, insignificance, purposelessness, hopelessness, and inadequacy with "W.W.N." kept me idle but was bound to explode. My fraternity would sing a song about W.W.N.—wine, women, and neckbones. Just like my granddaddy, I devoured wine (liquor, beer, Ray Hard, etc.) and women like I was eating a neckbone—lots of work for little meat, lots of bones, but still hungry when done. I was chasing, manipulating, and "playing" girls and justifying it by establishing common ground rules—my philosophy. "I am not looking for a commitment," was the foundational truth in that philosophy. Put in terms of the times, I was a "player." People said that I had "game." I manipulated and broke a few hearts before I discovered mine. In between all of the playing, I was drowning... in myself, in lies, and in the game. I was truly being what I saw. College became more about being a buck than about being great. I was being like Granddaddy and like most men I knew growing up. I fulfilled what was expected of men, especially black men. The man at my friend Chris's church was right about me. I did not fall far from the tree. I was the young buck of a well-known stag. At times in my life, it was a good idea for men to grab their daughters and "hide'em," like the man suggested. Now, I have a daughter entering college and I pray that she when she meets the likes of the old me, she will recognize that player and the dysfunction that was in my mirror.

To add to my misery or to my running from God, I too found

myself in front of a judge after getting into a fight. Like my nephew after Pops' passing, I was seeing what I was being—certainly not making his name great. Like him, my powdered keg of dysfunction finally exploded. Regretfully, I lost control and got into a fight. Although charges were dropped, I was ashamed as Mom, Aunt Doris, and my sister Shari sat and watched in the courtroom. The light of our family's supposed shining star had dimmed. Everything about that leader in the mirror was fleeting. That leader in my mirror could no longer be trusted and could no longer be followed. The leader in my mirror was no longer the best our family had to offer, was no longer fit for our family to present as first fruits, was no longer different from the rest of the world, and was no longer the oxymoron.

I was just a moron from L.A.; garnering fleeting trust and fleeting discipleship. I was a dysfunctional leader with a bad concussion, with no anchor, no identity, no purpose, no coverage, and out of season. I can finally see why and how lost souls with identity crises are recruited to join causes or purposes that offer significance, power, a place, a history, a future. But I thank God for not giving up on me. God had sent me some shake-up calls; nevertheless, He also sent me an angel who I did not deserve and surely was not ready for.

Chapter 4:
ADVOCATE LEADERSHIP

CUE LEADERSHIP MATRIX©

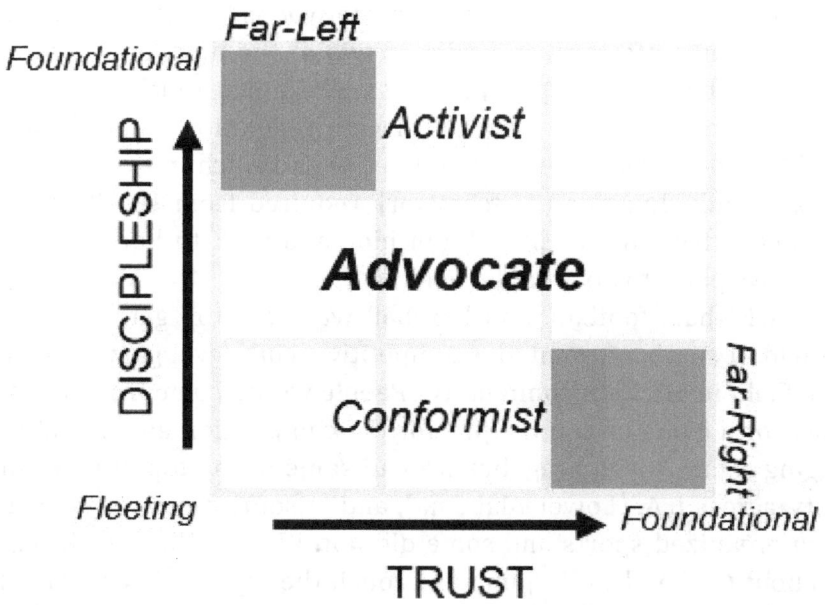

"I got Eric!"
—Jody

Participation in club sports has become a "must" for today's amateur athletes, especially if a kid truly wants to hone in on fundamentals, play with the best competition, and grow as an athlete. Unfortunately, it is also extremely expensive, making it a burden for most parents. It definitely would have been for my parents. I thank God for my athletic ability, but I also thank God for "The Field." The Field was essentially that; a 60 yard by 20 yard dirt surface in the middle of the community where we all played. Two of our neighbors sacrificed a portion of their acre of land used mostly to plant gardens for us to have

Chapter 4: Advocate Leadership

a gathering place.

The Field was our playground with no playground equipment, no court boundary lines, no referees, and no shortages of top athletes. We also called it the "red-top" because of the red clay surface that's prevalent throughout the south. The playground sported only one street light, a basketball goal, and our imagination.

Keeping that basketball goal usable was a journey of hard work. We would find a nice straight tree in the woods, cut it down with axe, shave the limbs off, carry it a mile or two to the field, dig a deep hole, build a backboard using plywood or small planks, attach a rim, set the post with water and red clay, and have a regulation height basketball goal. The older brothers, who had jobs, would pitch in to buy the rims, nets, and balls. Imagine the teamwork required from 10-12 of us who harvested a tree just to play. From hide-and-seek to hopscotch, there was always place to do it on the field.

Basketball, football, and baseball were the top games played on the Field. If someone wanted a competitive, club-level game, they came to the Field in Mt. Zion community. People would come from across the county for a game of hoops—just for the competition and of course the bragging right. Not to brag, but we had some of the top athletes in our county, across L.A. (Lower Alabama), and in some cases the state. Some played organized sports and some did not. We had Vince Jackson, who was about 6'3" and could jump and touch the top of a backboard. Then there was Paul McDole, known as "Buckwheat," who was left-handed and could catch a ball using a right-hand glove (on his throwing hand), switch off the glove, and make a throw faster than most right-handed throwers. We had speedsters like Curtis Peterson, who we saw with our own eyes catch a rabbit. It was pure genius when Curtis guessed the rabbit's next move and reached down and clipped its hind legs. The rabbit tumbled forward, regained its balance, and scampered away. I would not share if I had not seen it for myself while a group of us were walking through the woods. Curtis, known as "Curty Cat," added to his legend that day and remained a legend as he became a state 100-meter champion. But he lives in infamy for a 100-yard kick-off return in the State 5A Football Championship game in 1987 to tie the game. Curty Cat scampered untouched in a straight line down the middle of the field with only 10 seconds rolling off the clock. Our community produced record holders and athletic scholarship recipients in many sports, because the Field was our club and training ground.

We had many more like Vince, Curty Cat, and Buckwheat including my brothers, Tom III (TP or Tom-Tom) and Ronald Edward (Jody). Tom held rushing records for Greenville High, was All-SEC and a Pre-Season All-American strong safety at Auburn, and signed with the Tampa Bay Buccaneers. Not just because he is my brother, I believe he was one of the best—he could cover like a corner and hit like a linebacker. Tom is a legend, embedded in the fabric of our community. He was our hometown's first major star, and was recruited by all the major colleges from coast to coast. How often does someone have Coach Pat Dye of Auburn and Coach Paul "Bear" Bryant in your 500 square-foot home on the same day? Going to Auburn all those years was life changing. It opened my eyes to another world.

We had some good times at those games, watching the likes of Vincent "Bo" Jackson, "Little Train" Lionel James, Kevin Green, Tommie Agee, Andre Bruce, and others. I loved to watch the "mutant" that was Bo Jackson, but watching Lionel James play at that level boosted my confidence to believe that I could as well.

My favorite was always my own brother. Tom was the real deal and inspired us and many generations of players after that. A dear teacher and Auburn alum, Mrs. Linda Pierce, attended a local Auburn Alumni meeting with her husband, Tim, held during Tom's second year at Auburn. Mr. Peirce asked the guest speaker, David Housel, how Tom was doing. She paraphrased David's reply: "If you had a mold for the prototypical strong safety and you cracked it open, Tommy Powell would step out."

It was difficult for me to explain how big of a deal Tom was to my wife until she saw it for herself. Tai and I were having lunch with Tom and his wife Nancy at a restaurant last year. Strangely, I thought I saw a white gentleman in his late forties snap a picture of us with his phone. He continued to stare, and others in his party looked back at us as well. No one but me seemed to notice. Then, as the gentleman and his group began to leave, he stopped by the table with a curious and excited look on his face. Asking us to forgive his interruption, he inquired, "Are you Tommy Powell?"

Tom said, "Yes, how are you?" The gentlemen seemed to jump out

Chapter 4: Advocate Leadership

of his shoes and shouted to his friends, "I told y'all it was him!" He said, "Man, we are your biggest fans. We watched you when you were at Auburn. You were dynamite! My folks are not going to believe that I saw you today!"

He and Tom had a nice brief chat about Tom's injury during his senior year, about Tom is doing now, and about the hopes for Auburn this year. Tai was astounded, not just at the fact this middle-aged man was acting this way, but that it happened almost 30 years later. Tom was awesome!

He was a great big brother, and Jody and I wanted to be him, literally. Tom's #9 jersey was the only jersey that Jody or I have worn in public, other than my own. Not to get too sentimental, but my best memories are of Tom finding us during the Tiger Walk before the game, giving us a thumbs up during pre-game warm-ups, and making it through a crowd of fans (autographs, pictures, or conversations) just to get to us first. He was at true coach—a motivator and a doer. He showed us how to prepare—physically and mentally—for competition during the season and off-season.

He motivated us by stressing that there was nothing we could not do and that we could win at anything. One of the biggest compliments that he paid me was in front of his teammates that made up their All-SEC secondary at Auburn. It was before one of my little league baseball games, and I overheard him tell his teammates, who were home with him for the weekend, that they had to go to my game before they "hit the town." One them asked, "TP, is he any good?"

Tom said, "Let me put it this way. Nine of him would beat nine of us in baseball."

Do you know what that did to the mind of this 12 year old? His body of work was tough to follow.

But my brother Jody did follow. Jody was one those guys who could do it all—play point guard on anyone's basketball team, throw a fastball at low to mid-90s speeds, throw a football 60-70 yards flat-footed, or play anything else (putt-putt, bowling, archery, punt, horse shoes...). He was the quarterback for our high school when we won our first state championship in 1987 and was the 5A State Player of the Year in 1987 and first team All-State in both his junior and senior years. He got that state ring that eluded Tom and me. His record as a starter was

28-1. He was recruited by the big schools, but lacked the grades due to the Prop 48 rules that began in 1986.

Jody signed at the University of North Alabama (UNA). Jody was a phenomenal athlete, but he would be the first to share that he did not focus on academics like he should have. So, he left UNA for Hines Community College in Mississippi and led them to the junior college title game. Jody's risk-taking caused him to make both good choices and bad ones. Even in his bad decisions, he managed to get yet another lifeline, another opportunity, or another chance. In the midst of struggling after a failed career and failing marriage, he got another shot to try to fulfill "what could have been."

Jody actually earned the chance to try out for Major League Baseball at age 35. He had lost a step or two, but had not lost his strong and accurate arm. He made a few cuts but did not make it in the end. Even so, he was quite the athlete! He seemed to have nine lives, but he was always more concerned about me than he was about achieving greatness.

Needless to say, my two brothers cast a shadow of legendary status, and I was expected to do the same regardless that I was just 5 foot nothing. They left big shoes to fill, both on and off the field of play. Being the last of nine children, I had advocates all around me. Especially Jody.

Jody and I were closer in age and spent more time together than I did with the others, whether it was playing on the Field or playing "hard-strike-out." Hard-strike-out was one on one baseball. All we needed was a tennis ball, a bat or broom stick, and a wall. With one batter and one pitcher, the only rule was that the pitcher could not bat until he struck out the batter. The side of our house was the catcher. Needless to say, I spent a lot time pitching until I grew older.

If not for Jody, I would have been simply a nerd. He forced me to get out of my shell. Jody was a pure rebel, daredevil, and would try anything at least once. Being adventurous, Jody got into trouble because of things he did as well as for things *I* did. He took the most, if not all of the blame, even if I was at fault. Plus, he knew that Dad held us accountable for each other. Even after I told Mom or Dad that I was at fault, Jody had a way placing the blame on himself. He had a special way with Mom and Dad and with people in general. He could talk to anyone

Chapter 4: Advocate Leadership

and get them to open up or to follow him. He was a captain—on and off the field.

Jody had a way with the ladies, and he always had a stable of girls in waiting. When I became more interested in girls, I followed him and played the cute, cool younger brother. His friends were my friends. He covered me.

We had many good times, but some of the best times were on the Field. Since Jody was always captain, I always played. Among all of my fond memories, one thing sticks out. No matter what the competition, no matter the available talent, no matter the size or age of those available, Jody always picked me first. I loved to hear, "I got Eric!" Hearing those words felt better every time. Even when I was not ready and had not matured enough to compete, I was always his first pick. He knew I was not ready, but he forced me to play up. If we were playing basketball, he assigned me to the point guard. Jody would tap me on the butt and say, "C'mon now. You can do it... Don't let him breathe!"

It did not matter that I did not have a good jump shot. He used what I had, which was my defense—speed, quickness, and hustle. If we had a statistician for sandlot sports, I would probably be one of the leaders in all-time steals for basketball and baseball, football interceptions, inside-the-park homeruns, homerun saving catches (we had no fence), and run-downs (saving a home run or saving a touchdown). Who needed a club coach when I had Jody? He was my club coach and would get mad when he saw me playing against my friends that were the same age or younger.

"I don't want you playing with those scrubs," he would say. Of course, I did not listen. But I listened for those words: "I got Eric!" Every time that he said it, he invested in me; he showed patience with me; he empowered me; he honored me; he nurtured me; he stretched me; he grew my confidence; and he made me compete by playing up. When I became stronger and faster (not bigger), my confidence levels and performance accelerated off the charts. He was and still is a Brother's Keeper because he put himself second and showed me how to be one-to-another—how to ensure the wellness of someone else.

Jody knew how to motivate people, especially me. Early in our childhood, he used dares. All he had to do was dare me, and just like most little brothers, I would do it, no matter what *it* was. Dad knew this.

That is why he made Jody responsible for my actions. If I got in trouble, so did Jody. So Jody moved from motivating with dares to motivating me with challenges by saying that "I was too small" to do something. He had me for years on that one. Then after forcing me to play up and preparing me, he moved to being my "hype man." He told me that I was going to be better than him, and reinforced, "No one can be tougher than you."

When we visited new places, he would use me to hustle a few games of two-on-two. He could sell anything. Willing opponents would look at how small I was and bet Jody their week's lunch money that they could beat Jody and me. They did so not realizing that they could not keep up with my quickness and that I could jump above the rim. My part of the strategy was to never stop moving. Once I cleared out the middle, he would drive and take his defender to the basket. He penetrated, and I would follow and crash the board for a potential rebound. When the defenders adjusted, the one guarding me would become too tired of chasing me, and the pass lanes opened up from Jody to me. It was beautiful. Most of the time we would win because of our strategy, but mostly our wins came because of our chemistry. We had played so much together, we knew what each other was thinking by just looking at each other. We used to get accused of cheating cards, but we could simply read each other. Being hustled would get under our opponents' skin and did not go over well. Jody had a real knack of getting under people's skin. He somehow knew what buttons to push, no matter whose they were; and this included our dad's. There were times Jody would purposely run interference or pick a conflict with Dad to ensure that Dad's wrath focused on him instead of anyone else.

Most of all, Jody loved to have fun. He was the life of the party no matter where he went, whether at school dance or the hole-in-the-wall juke joint. On Fridays, we would drop off my Dad to meet his buddies at the "First Chance, Last Chance" so that we could use his car for the night. The sign at the juke joint had "First Chance" written on the front door and "Last Chance" written on the back of the door to be seen when leaving. Both sides enticed visitors to stay. Before we'd leave, Jody always hit the dance floor. And, as always, a group of ladies who were regulars would follow him onto the floor. It was a sight to see five to six voluptuous ladies circling Jody and waiting for their chance to dance.

Sometimes, Jody went too far with his fun, like the time I heard

Chapter 4: Advocate Leadership

him screaming my name from outside like it was life-or-death. I ignored him initially because he sounded too believable and I was not falling for his tricks again. He persisted. I heard him scream, "Eric! Help! Help! Help Eric, help!"

I would not budge and was not falling for it. Then my sister asked me, "Will you go to that fool?"

I relented. When I opened the back door, all I could see was our backyard ablaze with fire! There were towers of fire, spreading faster than Jody could put out. The dried up kudzu in our backyard, clinging to the fence and to the pasture, and climbing up an old oak tree made excellent tinder. Kudzu is a type of clinging, trailing, perennial vine that covered much of the south. In our backyard it covered from the fence out to the pasture, and climbed up an old oak tree. We had a humongous, out-of-control brushfire! I thank God that the wind was blowing west, because our home and our neighbor's home would have been set ablaze. I ran out and screamed to him to grab Dad's work clothes (tough Wrangler jeans) off the clothesline. I yelled to my sister Pat to call the volunteer fire department, I screamed back to Jody to take the left (south) side and I took the right to make sure that the fire would not burn the corn field on his side or the neighborhood on my side. Jody shouted, "What about the middle?" I exclaimed to just let it burn to the pond. The choice was to either let the neighborhood burn or let the grass and trees burn on the land that belong to the Fails family. We let the middle burn toward the pond, which was about 100 yards behind our house. Considering the circumstance, it seemed the most reasonable call. It felt like we fought that fire for hours. When I almost passed out from the smoke, I prayed to God for strength and asked for His grace, for surely my life was not to end fighting a bushfire as a teenager. We were exhausted. As we got the fire under control, our volunteer fire department finally showed. They did nothing but hand me a fire flap. Then I asked, "Are you guys gonna help?" They then pulled their truck up and sprayed water in a few spots.

The fire was out. Everyone was safe. All homes were intact. What happened next? By that time, Dad had made it home and knew exactly what happened. He went straight to Jody to make sure he was OK, and then he asked in his matter-of-fact voice, "Didn't I tell ya' to watch that dam' fire and not to leave it by itself?"

Jody had no answer. We did not have trash or garbage pickup in the rural areas. Everyone burned their trash, either in a trash pile or a 55-gallon steel drum. Jody was burning the trash, and did not tend to it as Dad has always told us. Dad had stressed that Jody had to tend to the fire that day because the wind was blowing high. Now, Dad had to go talk to Mrs. Gertrude Fails about burning up about 5 acres of her land. Thankfully, she was not angry, and was actually glad because she was needing to do a controlled burn. A controlled burn is an intentional, controlled fire to: 1. reduce the build-up of deadwood, overcrowded, and unhealthy trees; 2. prepare the land for new growth to allow for nitrogen and other nutrients to release into the soil; and 3. help plants and trees to germinate and regenerate.

To draw a parallel, Jody was that fire to me, he protected me from unhealthy things; he pushed me to be prepared and sharp—physically, mentally, and spiritually; and he planted seeds of himself to me in order for me to do the same for my nephews, cousins, friends, and all whom I come across. Proverbs 27:17 shares, "As iron sharpens iron, so one person sharpens another." Jody was iron for me, like my older brother Tom was iron for both him and me, and like Dad was iron for all three of us. Jody was my advocate for my well-being. Regardless of what shortcomings we both had, he placed me before himself.

But that was true of all in our family and community—the Village. Advocating for the future was what our community was all about. People in our community truly tried to sharpen us through love and serving one another and hold us accountable to do the same. From church, neighbor, friends, and community, everyone earned the right to ensure that our generation be one-to-another. If we were misbehaving, adults would scold or discipline us, tell our parents, and encourage us to do better. When Buckwheat saw Mom coming, he would run and hide because he could not lie her about behaving on the school bus or in school. Ms. Mattie Frost read the honor list every six weeks at Sunday school. If one of our names was not on it, we had to face and answer to the community. It was tougher for me (and others) because if my name was not called on the "A" honor roll, I had droves of adults darting at me after dismissal. I and others had set that expectation and were expected to tutor and help those that did not make it. Expectations. There were advocates for us at home, church, on the school bus, wherever you could

Chapter 4: Advocate Leadership

imagine. We did not need Twitter because things went viral through the old social media called party lines. If we misbehaved, someone in our family knew before you got home. The worst thing was if Mom or Dad heard about it at work or in public. That was bad news! But when we accomplished good things (honor roll, new job, drug rehab, prison release, etc.), we got praise and encouragement from everyone—sharpening iron. Our Village had all our backs.

John 13:34-35 shares, "A new command I give you: Love one another. As I have loved you, so you must love one another. By this everyone will know that you are my disciples, if you love one another." Christ calls us to be one-to-another, and we cherished that while growing up. I do not long for the past, but it seems that we are missing this today—advocating for the next generation. In God's will the future was their purpose and was foundational in all who supported it. The question is... in this Me-Now generation is it our purpose too? Are we leading for the future? Are we advocating for it? If not, what are we advocating for?

What happens when influential leaders advocate for a philosophy or perceived change by a great speech or great politics? True leadership is the ability to garner trust and discipleship, i.e., convincing people to trust and follow. But true transformational leadership is the ability to garner trust and discipleship that is purposeful and foundational. We have varying types of leadership that range from totally dysfunctional to transformational attributes. Sadly, this has led and is leading to fleeting unsustainable change. Most of today's visible leaders have self-imposed weights of gamesmanship and philosophy that scale back their ability to be transformational. Gamesmanship and philosophy impedes purposeful and foundational change that the nation and future generations need. The change we need should foster and cultivate things that are of God; not of self, the world, or some doctrine. Instead of the viral nature of love from the party lines, today's viral culture seems to have no interest in elevating the hearts, minds, and spirits of those they serve. Today's advocate leaders have had great intentions but have left those they lead with the inability to cope during crisis. Not having the goal of growth in mind, they have incited an ill-informed mass of people around their circumstances or created victims based on ideas and positions that are not their own. Admittedly, the most visible advocate leaders definitely have the pulse of the people, but thrive in the chaos that keeps our Societal Ecosystem out of balance.

Advocate leaders reside on both ends of the political spectrum—the Far-Right and the Far-Left America. Their thirst for power and thrust for influence tips the leadership scale, hindering their ability to build foundational trust and discipleship because they are over-weighted by gamesmanship or philosophy. Both have been effective in maintaining the viability of their principles and politics, but have kept people in the smoky haze of a brush fire of division. How does the leader in the mirror know if he or she is an advocate leader—a leader inspiring change for singular power, cause, or philosophy?

Far-Left Advocates

Often using any available medium or stomp to share their message, these leaders are heavy on gamesmanship to build foundational discipleship. They need a crisis (usually one that has been conveniently ignored) and a mass of followers in demonstration to sustain their approach. The Far-Left Advocate strongly desires change no matter the cost, and is a scout on a constant mission for the next issue, while often avoiding real solutions. They try and land on the side of the right. They carry labels such as autocratic, tolerant, extremist, activist, die-hard, manic, or radical. These leaders game the system to maintain power by inciting the masses and stealthily admiring chaos created from causes like racism, poverty, wealth transfer, and same-sex marriages—inequality. Depending on self rather than a higher power, Far-Left Advocates use gamesmanship to build blind discipleship and at times, change like a chameleon to suit the situation. If there is a "majority" in anything, Far-Left Advocates will fight against that majority based on race, religion, sex, holy marriage, wealth, or whatever they grasp onto. As an example, most black folks I know are religious conservative and object to same-sex marriage. The broad term "inequality" is a brilliant catch-all phrase. Far-Left Advocates are forced to be idle and silent to ensure that they not disrupt the inequality machine. If they share their true principles and positions on this, it will upset the "racism" pillar of the inequality machine. That is misplaced loyalty at its best. If a black person or a person from any social-economic disadvantage objects or does not pledge his/her loyalty to the

Chapter 4: Advocate Leadership

inequality machine, that person is shamed or intimidated with agents who use words like "sell-out, Oreo, Uncle Tom or out of touch."

A family friend, who is a retired sociology professor, often talks about having "Logic in Utility." A utility is the system, processes, and resources that support a defined purpose. That purpose has to:
- grow others,
- produce more individuals, and
- make an "Intellectual Leap" to improve a situation.

My friend shared, "If it has utility, it uplifts... If it does not, it diminishes..."

There is no utility logic in the leadership of most black advocate leaders. Under their helm, our Societal Ecosystem for America, black and non-black, has been diminished and damaged. This advocate leadership demonstrates the leader in the mirror harboring anger, unforgiveness, despair, envy, jealousy, and a need to be championed. Leader in the mirror, why foster unforgiveness? Haven't we been robbed and hustled enough by the inequality pimps?

Regardless of the answer, the so-called black leaders are still holding to the past and using the only utility they have: advocacy or activism:

1. Rally
2. March
3. Shake-down for money or pursue government action and
4. Be a pacifier for the leader and scraps for the followers.

Rally, March, Shake-Down, and Pacify. These leaders have perfected this utility, and this is all the leadership they know. Although the season for this leadership has past, these inequality pimps somehow remained relevant and still resonate with most black folks. But the utility has not moved Black America up the social-economic ladder. These tools have proven useless in uplifting but have proven valuable in supporting the inequality machine or narrative. This hypocrisy manifested in the supporting of Paula Deen who said the "N" word and the demonizing of Donald Sterling who did not say the "N" word.

I was caught up in that hypocrisy up until college. In the spring of 1994, after the acquittal of O.J. Simpson, almost every black student on campus poured out of the dorms and classrooms when the jury announced the "not guilty" verdict. The crowd was emotionally charged; not in anger but joy. I recall someone saying, "A black man beat The Man." Our campuses, our communities, and our nation were having this debate due to the historical treatment of blacks in America. Everyone was emotionally charged, especially after the racially-charged testimony of Los Angeles Police Detective Mark Fuhrman.

During that time, we had our own racially charged event on our campus around a student government race. Two white students were opposing each other in a race to head the student body. In a private conversation, the favored candidate supposedly said a racially charged comment to the less-favored candidate. The less-favored candidate shared that private conversation with some of the black student government leaders. The black student government leaders decided to demonstrate, demanded the favored candidate's resignation, and charged the office of the president of the university, Dr. Harold McGee, a man that I admired and respected. The group of black student leaders asked me to be a leader in this (and to bring the members of my fraternity and my black teammates). Without knowing all the story, I went with them and was right there in front... leading the charge.

Our university president was surprised, but agreed to speak with us. Once in the meeting, the advocate of our group demanded that Dr. McGee make the favored candidate resign from student government because of his comments. In his calm but deep voice, Dr. McGee asked, "What did he say?" As he asked the question, I realized at that moment that I had not asked that question either.

Our lead advocate then shared what the favored candidate said to the less-favored candidate. She said that the favored candidate told the less-favored candidate that he "sold out to the blacks" to get the the black votes.

Dr. McGee paused and said something piercing but simple. He asked the best question, "So what? Why is that causing all the demonstration?" Dr. McGee did not ask this arrogantly, but in a curious, confused, and profound way. As our leader began to explain, I stood up and walked out of Dr. McGee's office. I realized that Dr. McGee was right on with what he was inferring... it did not make sense. I realized that I had been hoodwinked and had jumped on a bandwagon advocating for

Chapter 4: Advocate Leadership

something without all the facts just because someone said that we should march. And my folks would not be proud. I was too hung up on "marching," like the prior generation had done. I was so ready to go back home and share how we marched into that president's office and "showed him that we were a force to be reckoned with." I wanted to make the elders in the Mt. Zion community proud and show that I too was taking the baton, being a drum major for justice. I was called a sell-out after walking out, especially after I went to the favored candidate (as I should have first) to talk to him. He was right. The less-favored candidate had sold out by trying to talk with "black" euphemisms, hanging with the blacks, speculating on who was probably racist in the student government, and doing special favors just to get the vote. The less-favored candidate had a smoking veil over the black leadership and could have said his own "I don't feel no ways tired" speech. Some tried to shame me when I stood up for the favored candidate and allowed him to say that he was my friend. I was not shamed by the black leaders but rather I was shamed because I was his friend (supposedly). I let emotion and a shallow rally cry shape an old utility: Rally, March, Shake-Down, and Pacify. I asked for forgiveness from the favored candidate and from Dr. McGee and thanked God for that awakening. I was an uninformed advocate using a useless utility; and I was not a credit to anyone.

Far-Right Advocates

Whether in Congress, on television, or on the radio, Far-Right Advocate leaders are easily identifiable, for they are guided by substantial and succinct philosophy that has built foundational trust among their followers. Prevalent tools and buzz words from these leaders are "free markets, low taxes, and morality." Focusing on allowing as little change as possible, Far-Right Advocates define themselves by a set of legacy traditions and principles and use an ideological philosophy to build blind trust among its disciples. In essence, these leaders are focused on maintaining the status-quo rather than enlightening people. Their principles make them so rigid that it hinders their ability to balance what is right versus what is reasonable. They err on the side of reasonable, which make them seem dogmatic and labeled as biased, racist, fanatic, redneck, sexist, bigot, unfair, discriminating. We have to careful about these labels especially when these words mislabel God-fearing, family men. There are times when these advocate leaders deserve some of this. Right on many prominent moral issues in America, the Far-Right fails miserably on the moral issues of race, poverty, and entitlement to God. Far-Right Advocates have not been immune to their own hypocrisy, i.e., self-unaware. They champion the moral issues of the day, but refuse to acknowledge the moral issues of racism, poverty, or the golden rule— "do unto others as you would have them do unto you." This hypocrisy manifested in justifying American slavery and ending food stamps. At the root of this hypocrisy is a hardened heart. The Far-Right wrapped the Lord around a hard set of principles, instead of wrapping their principles around God. That false wrapping gives them a sense of entitlement to God that all others cannot achieve. In other words, the false wrapping provides a false sense of security that God is on their side. Self-aware, President Abraham Lincoln understood this and did not allow that false security wrap him. He commented, "My concern is not whether God is on our side; my greatest concern is to be on God's side, for God is always right."

Where is that perspective in today's public forum? God is always right! To be fortunate enough to be on the right side of His will is what the leader in the mirror should pray for.

Confronting the reality that you may not be on the right side of His will is even more fortunate. I confronted that same reality last year. Tai and I decided to take the girls to Washington, DC for President Obama's second inauguration. I wrote this after the trip—

"Presidential Work-Out"

Our trip was a great experience and something that we will not forget. However, the only drawback was that we all got a workout. With the metro train taking us only so far, we seemed to walk for miles and stand packed in groups before finally making it through security. My wife Tai and I got an extra workout from carrying Karson, since strollers were not allowed around the capital. I am thankful that Kennedy and I had been training in her pre-track workouts, but the funny thing was that I got another type of workout... one that is spiritually based.

As we boarded the flight to DC on last Sunday, I sensed a different feeling growing and taking shape inside of me—a feeling of resolve, renewal, responsibility, and restlessness. Sharing the inauguration with my family and friends (in a chance meeting, we ran into Tai's college sorority sister, Ebun, exiting a building while we entered); watching people in the airport; talking to those young and old (even a renowned MLB manager); feeling their spirits; and seeing the peace in their eyes, ignited the feeling. I began to question my philosophies. What did God want me to see, hear, experience, or work out in my life?

As we walked on the mall, the feeling grew more as Tai and I talked about Dr. King, considering that he called for healing in our nation over 50 years ago in our nation's capitol. I believe that Dr. King's famous words had a deeper meaning than just being "free at last" from oppression of others. I believe that the message was more for the oppressors than for the oppressed. Dr. King could have been calling for the oppressor to "free, at last," their own hardened hearts. Hardened hearts prolong the march to freedom for the oppressed. Hardened hearts deny God-given rights—life, liberty, and the pursuit of happiness. Hardened hearts of the oppressors harden the hearts of the oppressed over the generations. Fast forward to today, on one end of the political spectrum, unforgiveness has a stronghold on the hearts of the oppressed's descendants. On the other end, the inability to be empathetic (walk in their shoes) has a hold on the hearts of the oppressor's descendants. I believe that hard hearts are at the root of the lack of healing and the seed of this nation's divide.

As we watched and listened to the President's speech, we realized that the theme was about the pursuit of equality—in opportunity, in jobs, in taxes, in the military, and even in marriage. When he spoke of the latter, the next question for me was: Is the pursuit of absolute equality necessary regardless of the desire to honor God? The quick answer for most may be "yes." I would then ask if all desires honor God and who gets the glory... you, a benevolent cause, a benevolent government, or a benevolent God? My answer to what He wanted me to "work-out" began to form. As we were leaving the mall, the word "order" stuck with me. The Word of God teaches that everything has an order. Equality in the forms of legalistic-, self-, doctrinal-, worldly-desires are not in the front of the line ahead of God's sovereignty and dominion over us; our family, our community, our nation...

...Especially over me. Restless was the right word to describe me, until we were leaving Capitol Hill and nearing Union Station. Tai and I looked at each with a smile when we heard words to a familiar song. "When we can't sleep at night and we wonder why, may be God is trying to tell you something." Yes, people began to sing the signature song from *The Color Purple.* People being black folks and non-black. The song was not the "old Negro spiritual" that Dr. King hoped for, but it gave me a revelation that I was carrying weights of my own philosophies that were not aligned with my calling.

My politics have always been a little different than most (neither Democrat nor Republican but conservative-leaning). I used to prioritize my leaning by: 1. principles, 2. position, 3. personality, and then 4. politics. What I realized is that I had fitted God around the criteria #1—my own principle. I had masked my conservative leaning of having God on my side, instead of me being on His side. A major goal in CUE Leadership is to help leaders confront the reality of having these self-imposed weights (philosophy and gamesmanship) and to release the burden of these weights via spiritual workout. These workouts are based on the servant Nehemiah, who restored an exiled people back to the "promised land." My restlessness was an awakening that allowed me to lift these heavy weights to ensure that I remain restless for the Lord, restless to serve, restless to set our society on the course of reverence to God, restless for healing, restless in restoring an "exiled" God back to the conscience and promise of our nation.

That experience made me realize that I was a part of the problem. I was prancing around saying, "I got God" instead of praying that God would say, "I got Eric." My heart was hardened. It was the same hardened heart that drove the Ceasars, Persians, Romans, Hitlers, and Americas of the world. Hard hearts birthed Jim Crow, the Klan, and the Black Panthers. Sadly, hardened hearts also birthed the need for the Civil Rights Bill that granted rights that the Bill of Rights and the 13th amendment had already given to black people. Instead of listening to the

Chapter 4: Advocate Leadership

transformative leader, Frederick Douglass, our nation chose to give black people equal status under law (legal and civil rights), rather than giving black people equal status under God (divine and natural rights). This instrument of justice was so far reaching that is now at the root of this perverted order that exists in our Me-Now culture. If anyone can paint themselves as a victim under the law, they can sue for a civil rights violation because of race, color, religion, sex, or national origin. I am not being insensitive, and please don't take this in the wrong way. I benefited from it, but the list of the original five (race, color, religion, sex, or national origin) continues to expand in number and in meaning over someone's personal freedom and liberty to do what he or she wants (Me and right Now). There was a time where I wished that I could take this "shameful" black skin off. There was also a time when "good Christians" enslaved blacks and justified it with Scripture—the curse that God placed on Ham. Both had unintended consequences, but one fact could not change: I could never choose from being a Negro, having black skin, being a male, or descending from Africa.

Cursed or not, shamed or not, neither I nor the "good Christians" had realized and appreciated what Christ had truly done for the world. The Apostle Paul tells us in Galatians 5:1, "It is for Freedom that Christ has set us free. Stand firm then, and do not let yourselves be burdened again by a yoke of slavery." Freedom and liberty are not independent of God, no matter how free our freewill is. Is our freewill a license to do anything we want? Can we freelance outside the will of God just because the Civil Rights Bill of 1964 allows it? How to do we use freedom? Galatians 5:13 shares we are "called to be free. But do not use your freedom to indulge the sinful nature, rather, serve one another." Romans 8:2 talks about this as well: "For the law of the Spirit of life in Christ Jesus hath made me free from the law of sin and death." What the good Christians and I did not realize or appreciate was the fact that Jesus paid the price for us. We are now loose from the bonds, curses, shame, death, principalities, powers, or any other created thing. However, this freedom does not give us an excuse to give in to the desires of our own personal choices of the flesh or any other pleasures of self. Instead, we are to be like Christ and walk as He walked. Jesus went about His Father's business with a purpose—doing good and helping others. God's love calls us to do good and serve one another, not with a hardened heart but with a free heart.

Leader in the mirror, have a free heart to help people because your life is not about you right now but about giving the Lord the Glory and to serve others, not yourself. Love and surrender is the call, which permeated through Dr. King's calling and purpose not to pass the Civil Rights Act of 1964. Loving God, surrendering to His will, and being obedient to the call that He has placed on each and every one of us frees us to step out of the darkness of own our sinful urges and into His marvelous and Holy light.

Granted, the urges that accompany us in this life are strong and lead to unintended consequences under the guise of civil rights. These unintended consequences place a person's "freedom" to choose to do something in opposition of God's divine pronouncement. Leader in the mirror, we are not to be equally yoked to doctrine, including the Civil Rights Bill. The urges feel good or feel like a blessing, but freedom not anchored in Christ is a burden. Then we may enter a freefall to damnation because we advocate (maintain and defend) it at all costs in the name of freedom. What happens when what these civil rights facilitate places an entire nation under someone's personal urge and we choose to go against God's divine pronouncement? Is the person, the nation, or both called to account before God?

Leader in the mirror, ask yourself that. Be careful what you advocate for and who you follow. Too often, we label these advocate leaders as transforming society, instead they are stagnating society with a perpetual set of unintended consequences. Neither Far-Left Advocate leaders, Far-Right Advocate leaders, nor I can become truly transformational without migrating our perspectives.

Building discipleship by exciting emotion and guilt, the Far-Left should move to a point of reverence to things that are more important than themselves and release the weights of gamesmanship (power and causes). In contrast, building trust by framing logic through an ideology and duty, the Far-Right should move beyond their philosophy for greater good and release the weights of philosophy (ideology and tradition). In both causes, self-imposed weights laced with judgment of others hinders their ability to be truly transformational.

Whether on the Far-Right or the Far-Left, Advocate leaders use their leadership utilities to seize every lawful institution that man has created. In doing so, they can transform an event, word, or circumstance into an advantage to make more disciples in growing their sphere of

Chapter 4: Advocate Leadership

influence. Their disciple-making can birth some powerful forces that can easily become a kingdom to the leaders rather than a powerful force for the good of their followers (as well as for God's glory). Leader in the mirror, be aware that this disciple-making and the toxins of I.D.L.E.ness are the two major ingredients that keeps our Societal Ecosystem out of balance and with open gaps.

There is much to manage in today's society, but how impactful would it be if we could harness the foundational trust and discipleship that these advocates evoke? In this, we can decelerate the growth of viral politics and can herd this I.D.L.E. chaos into a cohesive approach to solve real problems. Yes, this idealistic, but this idealistic notion calls for transformational leaders, who can provide clarity and author a new course of which the next generations can be proud. However, cultivating sustainable good for society cannot be accomplished by mere humanly means. All leaders become transformational when they align their perspectives with a power higher than their own and with purpose that is far greater than their narratives and strategic agendas. These narratives and agendas, on both sides, currently stray away from and dismiss the higher power that is in God Almighty. Most historical leaders that society considers transformational embrace God—Lincoln, Dr. King, JFK, for example. However, the notion of separation of church and state has somehow viraled into separation of God and state, God and economics, God and education, and God and social/culture. Was the separation of church and state what the founders of our great nation intended or was it a part of their guiding principles of everyone having the freedom of his/her religion? God has judged people as well as nations throughout history. What makes us think that He has stopped? No one or no nation is exempt. If we think we are, let's test it...

- Can common good, agnostic of God, be sustainable?
- Is it really possible or prudent to separate the pursuit of common good from God?
- Does the above notion enter the thoughts and minds of leaders when they visit churches, synagogues, mosques, or temples with their families?
- Do my civil rights trump God?
- Is religion and God one in the same?

If the answers to all are affirmative, our society is irreverent to God's presence, power, dominion, love, and wrath. We need the leader in the mirror to realize the imbalance of our Societal Ecosystem and to understand the gaps and interdependencies as well as the "order" of things. You need the leader in the mirror restless to solve issues in society, not to be a perpetual advocate in a state of never-ending restlessness trying to grow power, causes, ideology, or tradition. Another way to put it: How does the leader in the mirror reduce the heavy build-up of philosophy and gamesmanship, prepare for new growth anchored in God's abundant soil, and allow for new growth and new fruit of the Spirit?

How do you ensure that God says, "I got the leader in the mirror"?

Chapter 5: STEWARD LEADERSHIP

CUE LEADERSHIP MATRIX©

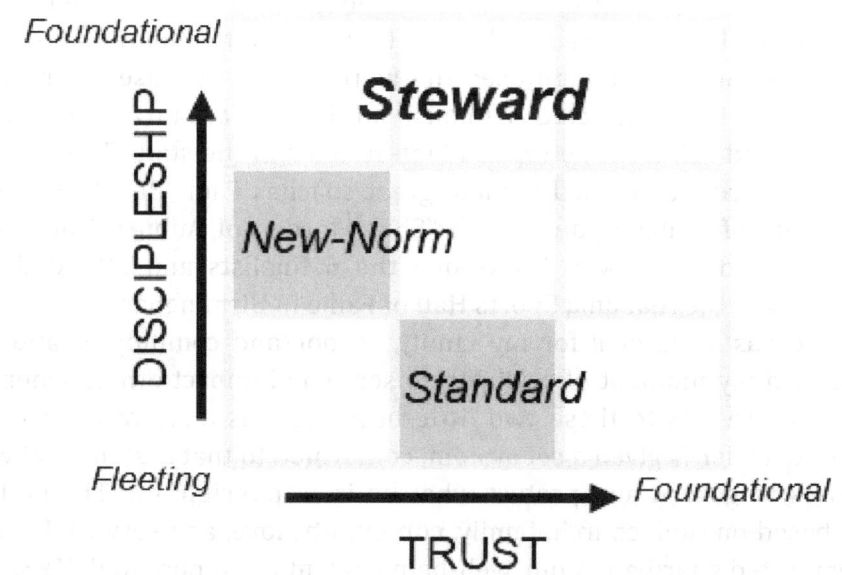

> "Are you being a good boy scout?"
> —Mr. Seth

"Mo'ning T'Derik, you did a good on T.V. last night," said Mr. Seth Lee Williams as I stepped on bus #30 to school. I smiled and thanked him. A family man, local farmer, and church steward, Mr. Seth was one of the community's school bus drivers and also my brother Tom's father-in-law. He called me T'Derik (even to this day), not in malicious way but an endearing way. I was not assigned to his bus, but it picked up later and dropped off earlier than the bus I was assigned to. As I got to high school, it made more sense to me to sleep later and come home earlier.

Chapter 5: Steward Leadership

On that morning, Mr. Seth was complimenting me on the T.V. interview for being honored as the WAKA-Church's Chicken Scholar Athlete of the Year. WAKA-TV, the local CBS affiliate, partnered with Church's Chicken to honor and select the top scholar-athlete in the southern region of Alabama. While keeping the stop sign out, Mr. Seth went on share, "You made us proud once again," expressing how proud the community was of me. In his classic way, Mr. Seth asked me to serve as he always did. He asked me to talk with two of the kids who got in trouble on the bus the day before. He used me and others in that way on the bus, at church, or in the community. Mr. Seth used the word "again" because during that same week I was selected a finalist for Bryant-Jordan Award, which honored and selected the top student-athletes in the state. The Bryant-Jordan Award was named for late great coaches Paul "Bear" Bryant of University of Alabama and Ralph "Shug" Jordan of Auburn University. Although I did not win, I was one the 6 finalists and attended the ceremony at the Alabama Sports Hall of Fame in Birmingham.

It was a big deal for my family, school, and community, and Mr. Seth used my moment of celebrity to serve and impact others when he asked me to talk to these two little boys. He was a steward leader. A steward leader is given a set system, conformed to that system, and who chooses to govern and protect what he is responsible for. The system was based on God, church, family, community, love, and service. He was a committed guardian of our well-being, talents, and potential. He was a "substantial marine" on the bus, in the community, and in life. He did what he supposed, how it needed to be done, and did not stray away. Mr. Seth was not only a community bus driver, he was also the steward at our community church, Mt. Zion. He served the church by maintaining the facilities, grounds, and other operational duties just like he served kids, community, and his sphere of influence. There was no more good and humble person than Mr. Seth. He was truly the salt of the earth. Regrettably, he was often disrespected by kids on the bus and church leaders, who mistook humbleness for weakness. He farmed all of his life and was not fortunate enough to go to school as others in the community had. Mr. Seth demonstrated what it meant to turn the other cheek and prayed for those people who disrespected him. Humbleness and the Golden Rule were the fabric of his system of life: "Do unto others as you would have them do unto you." (Luke 6:31) Jesus shared this as a lesson about loving our enemies. Jesus shifted the conventional quid pro quo method of treating people. Rather than doing to others what they have done to us, we are to treat others the way we want them to treat us. His adversaries deserved worse than how Mr. Seth responded, but he lived by that rule. His ability to turn the other cheek was not weakness, but a strength that we all need.

When I saw Mr. Seth recently, he used the same line that he used on us as kids. He asked, "Are you still being a good Boy Scout?" It was as relevant then as it is now. The church was at the center of everything in our community including scouting—Brownies, Girl Scouts, 4-H, Crusaders, Cub Scouts, and Boy Scouts. The Boy Scouts of America was a key tool for our community to shape us as leaders and citizens, and Mr. Seth and the community expected us to adhere to what the Scout Oath stood for: *On my honor I will do my best to do my duty to God and my country and to obey the Scout Law; To help other people at all times; To keep myself physically strong, mentally awake, and morally straight.*

Mr. Seth was the ultimate Scout, for he was "trustworthy, loyal, helpful, friendly, courteous, kind, obedient, cheerful, thrifty, brave, clean, and reverent." His question to me was simple, but kept me on my toes. I too mistook his humbleness for weakness. I thought that he was too quick to subordinate to people he perceived had more education, more wealth, more intelligence, more status, more land to farm, better speech, better tractors, betters homes, or a closer deacon seat. His perceived inadequacies seemed to keep him under the thumb of the so-called elites in our community. As it is in most churches, there is a distinct separation between the lay people or common folk and the social-economic elite or powerful. I fell in the former category, but never accepted it as my reality or my future.

We have to understand if the powerful elite can match fear with data or circumstance, they can get lay people to trust them. If the powerful elite can match yearning for self-worth with a role for you in their solution, they can get you to follow them to the ends of the earth. If the powerful elite can match your perceived inadequacy with a veil of control, they can get you to conform… stay in your place. Steward leadership is absolutely needed to maintain these growing philosophies. The danger is in how they play the game. When one's gamesmanship feeds on fear, inadequacy, or yearning for self-worth, the steward leader

Chapter 5: Steward Leadership

(or any leader for that matter) can become toxic and bear toxic results. Leaders use any means to maintain their philosophies by gaming the hearts and minds. These strategies include guilt, shame, embarrassment, and manipulation. More specifically, stewards take stock in experts; others to speak for them, be their voice, and champion their causes. Once stewards find that expert, they become the expert's "amen corner." The expert does not have to be right but only convincing and sound smart… like when you hear someone with a British accent report the news. That expert can triangulate anecdotal evidence around fear, low self-worth, and inadequacies. Anecdotal evidence matched to either three of these can rule the masses, convincing people of a notion based on circumstantial or made-up evidence.

A good friend from my time at Booz was fondly nicknamed the Mad Frenchman. This characterization showed during a project where we performed a gap assessment of the planning and execution of offshore capital projects for a super major oil and gas company. After reviewing our hypothesis, storyline, structure, and data, he shared in his deep French accent, "Good start. Your work is directionally correct but fundamentally wrong." *Directionally correct but fundamentally wrong? What?* That was his way of telling us we were blowing smoke.

We had used anecdotal data mixed with benchmarking and interviews from experts across the globe to draw our conclusions without analyzing real, quality, clean, and creditable historical data to support our work. We put too much stock in the passionate experts from across the globe who had credibility, but also had their own agendas. His point was the anecdotal evidence that we used to triangulate around our conclusions put us in the right direction, but our conclusions were wrong for now until there was real fundamental evidence. Although that worked in some cases to convince some clients, the Mad Frenchman impressed upon us that this client prided itself in being the smartest based on data. We needed statistically sound data at key decision points in planning and execution. Why decision points? Decisions imply that the client had control, governance, or transparency to make a decision and to influence the outcome where value (cost, schedule, and quality) is created and destroyed. We could not get by with our normal of being "directionally correct" with pretty PowerPoint slides, but without real evidence. We could not ask them to take an intellectual leap over the gap. The client would pick apart any data that was not fundamentally sound. It was intellectually dishonest. After all, they had brought us in and removed the leading management consultant for doing what we had done up to that point. If we were to lead them and give them a return on investment in not one but two management consulting firms on the same problem, we had to be *more than* stewards. We could not take the same notion or narrative and spin in it another way.

Another example of this is seen in the global warming debate. Oh, I forgot. It's called "climate change" now. This isn't a debate, but the discussion on climate change provides a good example of how steward leaders can commit with passion and persistence to a cause or a narrative. Convincing people that man controls the earth's weather, climate, and nature takes guts and is bold, especially using anecdotal data to tell various stories. The narrative has changed from chlorofluorocarbon (CFC) depleting the ozone layer to global freezing in the 70s and 80s to global warming over the last decade or so. It's continued even after scientists from two expert institutions were found to have changed historical weather data to make the earth's weather seem warmer after the turn of the recent century. That was intellectually dishonest, yet we still hear the debate and continue to ask society to take an intellectual leap on the matter. Fudged data coupled with a persistent communication narrative placed a veil over the eyes of many. Think about the commercials showing a polar bear on a floating piece of Artic ice, taken during the summer. Ice melts in the summer, and polar bears can swim. Right? Before I'm labeled as a denier, skeptic, or anything else, I believe that we have to be *more than* good stewards of the earth and all of the vast resources God has given us and called us to as He gave us dominion over the earth. Using my own anecdotal evidence or notions, I believe that there has been exponentially more carbon-based emissions and particulates (bad stuff) released by volcano eruptions than the amount of bad stuff released in all of the Industrial Revolution since man has been building things. Remember Mount St. Helen or when volcanos in Iceland spewed tons of carbon and other toxic gases into the atmosphere? This cancelled all flights to and from Europe. Did man cause that earthly disruption?

That hypothesis is not backed by real data, but it has us thinking, *Huh?* Here is a biblically-based assertion from one of our other chapters:

Chapter 5: Steward Leadership

"Man cannot destroy what he did not have a hand in making." To kid ourselves that we have all the power in our hands to destroy what God has beautifully made and that God would stand by and allow us fools to do it is fundamentally wrong. (I look forward to that debate.)

We would think that the fudged data would make us question our position on the matter, but people doubled down by changing the narrative to "Climate Change" instead of changing our perspectives or getting another perspective or opinion, like our oil and gas client did. When we continue to hear a prominent statesman say, "Life as you know it on earth ends if climate deniers are wrong," we stewards should discern that that narrative is laced with fear. The most important thing for us to remember is that when the narrative becomes the mission, the leader has either a blurred vision, a masked vision (hidden agenda), or no vision at all. His/her steward leadership will conform and defend at all costs. Some lack logic and critical thinking or just refuse to use it because is about the "survival" of the narrative by finding new experts, tying to another issue (like national security), and feeding stewards a constant diet of communication using talking points. Without discernment, steward leaders can be trapped by a veil of ignorance because stewards often read only the headlines, will not ask the right questions, will repeat talking points like a parrot, and will cover the narrative just as volcano ash covered the Iceland sky.

These types of steward leaders are conformists and are the same type that passed out the yellow voting sheet in Mt. Zion to tell us who to vote for. These stewards do not need direction or approval from their ultimate leader, for they know the agenda and ensure plausible deniability for those they serve. This type of steward organizes the masses and devotes their expertise to a single area of work. They often have official titles such as director, adviser, or administrator. Most recently, they wear the name of "czar" and focus on issues. They are committed champions and are always willing to "fall on the sword," giving their leader some bottom-cover—loyalty for protection, plausible deniability, and scapegoats. Every leader needs loyal followers, but the question is how loyal is too loyal, especially around crisis time? When does loyalty become blind or create scales over followers' eyes? It would be interesting to investigate the correlation of the number of czars appointed to the level of presidential confidence; to approval ratings; to the number of mounting issues that nations or corporations face; or to the number of reorganizations a company or entity goes through in a given time. We have all have seen these stewards, perhaps in the mirror. They follow, emulate, and grow a veil or scales on their eyes. Stewards will rubber stamp anything the leaders want or hold the party line, even to the point of voting and passing one of the most historical landmark bills without even reading it. Regardless where you landed on the healthcare bill debate, if hearing the quote, "we have to pass the bill so you can find out what is in it," did not astound or give pause to the leader in the mirror, then the leader in the mirror has scales.

In 2 Timothy 4:3 we are warned that a time will come when people only hear what their "itching ears" want to hear. I believe we are living in that time. Godly leaders are warned that it is not to be that way among us.

If steward leaders are championing and conforming to the narrative and cause, they guard with attacks. There several ways to attack opponents, but one of the most effective utilities I have seen is leading by exception coupled with dismissive or passive aggression. Finding the exception not to do or to do something and being the smartest and loudest on that exception far too often rules decisions made. A recent example of that was how America dealt with unaccompanied kids from Central America. Can you imagine the circumstances and the despair that would drive a parent to send their child unaccompanied with the hope of saving of them? These people were risking and sacrificing their lives in search for a better life, in search for freedom, in search for the promise inscribed on the Statue of Liberty...

> 'Give me your tired, your poor,
> Your huddled masses yearning to breathe free,
> The wretched refuse of your teeming shore.
> Send these, the homeless, tempest-tossed, to me:
> I lift my lamp beside the golden door.'

There has been no better way of expressing that freedom than the Statue of Liberty. Can we express that same sentiment today? Does it remain true today? Was the "golden door" opened for the unaccompanied children from Central America or for anyone? No, it was

Chapter 5: Steward Leadership

not. The exception came in the narrative of illegal immigration and border security. The stewards against accepting these children were selective in their godly principles and in our motto "In God we trust."

What does the Word of God say about immigration? Leviticus 19:33-34 shares, "When a stranger sojourns with you in your land, you shall not do him wrong. You shall treat the stranger who sojourns with you as the native among you, and you shall love him as yourself, for you were strangers in the land of Egypt: I am the Lord your God." Did we do this? What does the Word of God say about children being sent, traded, or sold in a foreign land? Moses, who was left in a basket amid the reeds and bulrushes along the Nile in Egypt went on to free an entire people. Joseph was sold into slavery but saved a nation. Jesus was born into a damned world, but saves us all. Each of them has a purpose and along the way faced opposition from stewards with an agenda. In each instance, God frustrated the efforts of the stewards. Were the proponents of the border security selective on what was morally right? What was just as disappointing was that the proponents of taking care of these unaccompanied children had the power to act but conformed to what the opinion polls suggested: that the move would not be popular.

However, some stewards couple the exception tactic with passive aggressiveness that dismisses their proponent. We recognize this part of their utility by their indirect hostility. When we're stalling or procrastinating to make a decision or to act, there may be a good reason or a hidden agenda. It is effective, and I admit that I was a master of it for a long time. A stubbornness, refusal, or deliberate failure to act on a mandate or request for which one is responsible can destroy friendships, marriages, teams, or cultures. In my work, I have seen this in action too often (consultants are often the object of this). I had a couple of clients who suffered from having employees who led by exception coupled with passive aggressiveness. The utility was interwoven into their cultures because of diffused authority. Everyone had a say, anyone could reject what they didn't like, no one was held responsible, no one was accountable, and everyone blamed anyone. As an example, one client installed new IT systems to remove manual and paper-based processes, and improve work productivity. Employees had the autonomy *not* to use the new system. Management refused to make them use it, even after spending millions to deploy it, because it was not the culture to "impose mandates" on people. Problematic? Yes. It confused me, and still does in a sense.

However, the employees had good cause to revolt and use the culture to fight the new IT systems that were a part of a business transformation effort. The prior leadership tried to fix the problems with this business transformation effort, but failed at first CUE'ing up the business. With the intense culture to navigate, the leaders decided to go around the problem and needed someone who would take his/her lead verbatim, could do the work, and take the blame if things went wrong... a steward, a consultant. The leader directed the consultants to design the new system for how things should work and implement it as soon as possible. It should make you cringe to hear that. No wonder the employees revolted. They had no stake in the transformation, were not asked about the real problems, received no training, and were expected to use the new systems. To make matters worse, the consultants launched the system without a pilot to test operability. Employees had no ownership in closing their individual gaps. Leadership had good intentions, but this was a disaster to the point that the word "transformation" became a culturally sensitive word that sparked much emotion just from the sound of it.

Cultural sensitivity was the first or main filter in making decisions. In other words, political correctness ruled the day and created this bureaucracy where nothing got done. Instead of focusing on the key operating challenges and engaging employees and other stakeholders, the leadership decided to hire consultants that were steward leaders; to spend political capital to push through procurement and justify the investment; to cast a broad, comprehensive, and clumsy solution; to use power to impose a mandate on employees. Does that sound familiar? No wonder they experienced accountability challenges, no wonder they reorganized six times in four years, no wonder they had mounds of new policies and controls, no wonder the merry-go-round of new leaders, no wonder the power grabs and in-fighting, no wonder the "shadow" employees (duplicate staff to recheck the rechecked work), no wonder the opposition to fixing (uncovering) the issues. Conformity that is matched with eye-opening narrative, with anecdotal evidence, with passive aggression, with political correctness, and with diffused accountability builds an imposing wall of bureaucracy over those the

Chapter 5: Steward Leadership

leader leads. This leadership utility causes nothing but chaos.

The center blocks that allow the powerful elite to control their sphere of influence and mobilize steward leaders are fear, self-worth, and inadequacy. In this season, steward leadership is the most vulnerable but the most critical to correct. With our dedication to govern, protect, and preserve what we are responsible for, or what we are told to do, steward leaders will defend that expert with their last breath. They do it, even it means quickly pointing out what's wrong with those who have a differing opinion as well as ridiculing to discredit the difference maker. What is the most astounding is that the powerful elite does not have to give the order. Stewards protect the narrative, project, or the master's kingdom at all costs. What if... ? What if stewards were protecting the kingdom of the true Master instead? Why don't most?

There are simple answers and there are complex answers. When we wrap fear, self-worth, and inadequacy in one word we get "survival." We examined it with Peter denying Christ three times; with Orpah leaving Naomi; with Moses listening to the 10 spies instead of 2; and with Shemaiah the priest urging Nehemiah to flee into the temple as Tobiah and Sanballat were out to kill him. In Nehemiah 6:10-14, Nehemiah visited Shemaiah. Shemaiah said, "Let us meet in the house of God, inside the temple, and let us close the temple doors, because men are coming to kill you—by night they are coming to kill you." But Nehemiah was a man with great discernment, which is one the key qualities that the Lord anointed in Nehemiah's transformational leadership. Nehemiah said, "Should a man like me run away? Or should one like me go into the temple to save his life? I will not go!" Nehemiah realized that God had not sent Shemaiah, but in fact Tobiah and Sanballat had hired him to try to intimidate him. It was forbidden for a layman to enter the temple. Nehemiah would have committed a sin, which would have given him a bad name and discredited Him. Shemaiah was a priest, a steward of the temple, but proposed a course of action that was contrary to God's word. He was a conformist but more of a recusant steward. Shemaiah refused to make an objection to Sanballat and refused to submit to the Lord's authority. Sometimes, people use God's word, resources, house, and word to accomplish the wrong thing. One of my good friends and a regular guest of our radio show (whose name happens to be Nehemiah) would describe Shemaiah's actions using an indefinite article instead of a definite article. He'd say he was sharing "a" word of God instead of "the" word of God with Nehemiah. The leader in the mirror must be able to discern between the two: what is of God and what is not? What is anecdotal and what is fact-based evidence?

Sanballat, governor of Samaria, was the powerful elite of Nehemiah's time and strongly opposed the rebuilding of the walls. He orchestrated Shemaiah's plot and other lies, deceit, and false accusations against Nehemiah to stop Nehemiah's called work. Sanballat rallied prominent leaders around his agenda like Tobias, governor of Transjordan, and Geshem with prominent business in lucrative spice trade. Sanballat's goal was to discourage and thwart the transformation, the rebuilding of the wall and the way of life. Sanballat used Tobiah and Geshem as his "experts" to support the narrative that Nehemiah was trying build a new kingdom. They used the utility of letters, lies, and politics to hinder, stop, and silence the rebuilding and even went as far to accuse Nehemiah of taking kick-backs in exchange for favors. Sanballat was a judgmental, mocking, blindsiding spirit that sometimes manifests itself as a humble sheep or steward or expert. Flowing in this spirit, this blindsiding opposition may have only the intention to tear down the figurative wall God is calling you to build.

If Nehemiah had wavered in the face of adversity, his leadership would have been discredited. The morale of the people would have plummeted. Steward leaders like Shemaiah should understand when not to run away and not to focus on saving his own life but focus on saving the future. There was as much at stake then as now in the Me-Now culture. Notice the difference between Mr. Seth and the rest of the referenced leaders, climate experts, politicians, consultants, and Shemaiah. Mr. Seth and the Mad Frenchman represent the "Standard Steward," one who conforms to historical, traditional, or conventional ways, behaviors, rules, etc. to build more trust in a set of principles. Many of us may equate or dismiss this type of leadership as being on the "Right" side of the American political landscape. We may even use the culturally sensitive label, "Tea Party." There are similarities as it relates to principles, but how they are different is that both Mr. Seth and the Mad Frenchman were called to a purpose greater than themselves. Mr. Seth is even more different in that his point of reverence, or his anchor,

Chapter 5: Steward Leadership

is God and his purpose is saving souls not taxes, money, or culture. What happens, though, when Standard Stewards are called to a greater purpose but attack with hostility? We experience intimidation, death, oppression, and domination from gangs, sects, groups, mobs, or rings who have hardened hearts—Bloods, Crips, al-Qaeda, Boko Haram, Jim Crow, Hamas, Ku Klux Klan, Nazis, etc.—all of which are predators, preying on the weak, young, helpless, or innocent. These predators force Standard Stewards to conform by threat, guilt, or unsaid consequences or implication of a secret or narrative that would cause much harm if leaked. Standard Stewards protect the person or secret at all costs, sometimes by just ignoring or failing to acknowledge the disservice, even when the secret is apparent. Exposing secrets can lift the veil on voter fraud, Watergate, warrantless surveillance, Iran-Contra, Tuskegee's syphilis experiment, as well as family secrets. A family's secret can be the worst to expose, for it may surprise, hurt, aggravate, or open wounds. Keeping secrets for the greater good or to keep harmony has some relevance, but it can create a false peace. What if it has caused much damage to many people? What if the person who has the secret has tried to redeem himself?

That was my dilemma when I was asked to lead a prayer at my uncle's funeral in the spring of 2014. My dilemma was praying for the soul of the family secret that no one talked about. There was an uncle who molested me when I was 4 years old. He molested others as well, but I will allow them to share their own testimony. That experience was the reason that I stopped talking for a long time.

Fast forward about 25 years, I was sitting at my cubicle at work, and without warning, I began to remember...

My uncle spent years in the U.S. Army. On the day that he returned home at the end of his career, I recalled my aunt driving him home with a large floor model television in the back seat of the car. We were playing in front of our home when they drove up. As he emerged from the car and headed toward the house, he gave me a smirk that, in that moment, had power over me. When I saw his smirk, details of what happened were blurry, but I remembered a frantic run home.

Then, the memory of a 6'5" shadow at the door of my grandmother's bedroom door hit me like a wave. As I would do, I was taking a nap at Grandma's house in her bed while my uncle was home on leave. I'm not sure if anyone else was in the house at the time, but he walked into the room with his white Pony sneakers, high tube socks, and basketball shorts. He had that same smirk on his face. To this day, the Lord mercifully spares me of most of the details of what happened in a suppressed or blocked memory. But I remember his soft hands on my back and soft voice that froze me into shock. When it was over, I got up and ran home. The fear, discomfort, pain, violation, shame, guilt, and helplessness consumed me. I ran to our bathroom, shut the door, and packed magazines underneath as a stopper because the bathroom door did not lock. Shamed, broken, and confused, I stayed in the bathroom for a long time trying to make sense of the fear, the blood in my stool, and all of my feelings. After about 30 minutes, Mom called to see if I was OK. I did not answer. She walked into the bathroom and saw blood in my stool. She asked if I was constipated and when I didn't answer, she assumed that was the case. I could not and did not tell her what happened or what may have happened or what didn't happen. I told her that my stomach and butt were hurting. She asked me to stoop over and slipped a suppository to soften my stool. I was scared, confused, and shocked, and I did not tell anyone. That was the uncle I knew, for he clearly had done it before—prey on the seemingly voiceless.

I could not stop weeping that day at work as all of this came flooding back to my memory. Imagine the entire floor of co-workers watching me cry uncontrollably. I thank God for my good boss/friend Clyde King, who was shocked, understood, talked me back to calm, and allowed me to take time off. Tai had to plead with me to keep me from driving to the place my uncle lived at that time and taking his life. She physically latched onto me like glue to prevent me from leaving and she begged me to think about our family. After a few days I calmed down. I finally understood the eerie feeling I got going into my grandmother's room or when I shook my uncle's soft hands over the years. Fear and anxiety would just overcome me when if I came close to her door. *"Why now Lord?"* I asked. I know why now. The Lord could not use me as He intended. That affected my manhood. It was at the root of my problems before that moment, when I walked around with an angry spirit and at the root of problems in my marriage, as a father, and as a friend to others. Can you imagine the depression? It was at the root of why I ran from problems, bill collectors, friends, and God. Running was easier

Chapter 5: Stewart Leadership

because I could justify it. I even avoided visiting Alabama and for years never spoke to him.

What my uncle meant for evil, the Lord had use for His good. The Lord had to remove the dirt from that covered wound in order to heal me. He had to use that brokenness to mold me and make me over in order to fill me with Himself and use me in this ministry. That experience began a process of softening my heart, testing my faith, forgiving others, and lifting weights of depression and shame. Why didn't I expose him? I am not sure, but I truly thought that only more hurt could come of it. So I fell in line with being a steward of the family secret. I asked the Lord to give me the words to expose him, but I never got them. Maybe I could not speak the "truth in love" as Ephesians 4 calls us to do or maybe it was because I was still being "tossed to and from by the waves and carried about by every wind" of my hardened heart.

The prayer I gave at my uncle's funeral was testament to how God can transform the leader in the mirror. I almost went off-script with a hardened prayer, but God took over my spirit to deliver words of forgiveness, healing, and redemption. Could the leader in the mirror stand and deliver a prayer about the life of a predator who had committed this violation? It was tough, especially when I heard a young man speak of this same uncle. I have no evidence, but my spirit told me that this teenager was violated too. God used it to free me once and for all. That experience has no control over me anymore. I too was a standard steward protecting the family's secret: A predator that preyed on the weak, young, helpless, and innocent. I don't know if or when he stopped preying, but I know that at some point he started praying. He came to me after I spoke at our family reunion and said, "I have to get back home now, but I thank you."

I thought he was referring to my speech and said, "You are welcome." He said, "No, thank you... Thank you... Thank you..." I acted confused at first, but then I realized that he could not ask for forgiveness. His "thank you" was his way of asking. He pulled my hand to his chest and would not let it go. Knowing what he wanted, I almost pressed him to ask, confess it, and drop on his knees to beg from his redemption. But I said, "We are good. All is forgiven... I forgave you a long time ago." He said his final "thank you" and released my hand. I was able to free my uncle because *I* was free. I was able to hold his hands in prayer as my Pops was leaving this world because *I* was free. I was able to visit and pray with him in the last weeks of his life because *I* was free.

I could have spoken up and not been a standard steward, but this testimony is pleading for a new normal when it comes to protecting secrets, regardless of the consequences. We needed steward leaders that represent the "New-Norm." The New-Norm conforms to the new normal, to a renaissance view, or to rebel and revolution in efforts to build more followers for the cause or for self. The New-Norm is defined by urbandictionary.com as "The current state of being after some dramatic change has transpired. What replaces the expected, usual, typical state after an event occurs. The new normal encourages one to deal with current situations rather than lamenting what could have been."

We can find appropriate application in each pillar of our Societal Ecosystem, but what is common among them is the cause for change. New-Norm stewards protect and champion change. In our change, however, we must be mindful not to change our anchor or point of reverence. When we do, we fail to realize what Ecclesiastes (1:9) shared, "What has been will be again, what has been done will be done again; there is nothing new under the sun." Without God as our point of reverence, we are amazed at our own human enlightenment or discovery and miss the fact that we are in seasons and lessons that apply from past and present seasons.

Let's test this "Standard" vs. "New-Norm" stewardship in the future with the leader in the mirror. There is no better forum to test this than during the State of the Union addresses. Instead of being separated by the House of Representatives and the Senate, our leaders are separated by party lines—"Standard" stewards on one side and "New-Norm" stewards on the other side. One side wants change, one side wants no change, and neither side wants a change in profession. Depending on what is said by the U.S. President, the majority of the substance in the address will receive cheers from the "amen corner" from the President's party and will receive groans from the "rival row." The rabid stance on party lines is symptomatic of the notion that we have more stewards representing the people and the states than any other type of leader. There are advocate leaders who control the "amen corner" and the "rival row" and who maintain the chaos that we see in

Chapter 5: Steward Leadership

the Me-Now culture. Those same advocate leaders controlled the client that I referenced on page 83.

We should call it the State of the Discord, State of the Separation, or the State of the Conformity, and the President should end the speech by saying, "the state of our discord is strong." Taking a page out of the steward leadership playbook, I will evoke an expert, a founder of this nation, John Adams. John Adams had few quotes on government. One of which he shared, "When legislature is corrupted, the people are undone." Is legislature corrupted? Are we undone? Are we scattered? Yes, sometimes "New-Norm" stewards take change too far and "Standard" stewards take principles too far. The extremes of both places strain on or warps our Societal Ecosystem because both have been disconnected from God. We can debate the "separation of church and state," but God and church is not a 1:1 ratio. To much current debate, Adams shared, "The government of the United States is not, in any sense, founded on the Christian religion." As much as we would like to believe it, is it true and was he right? I am sure we will get a few mental cheers from the leaders in the "amen corner." But on the "rival row" side, consider what John Adam shared, "Our Constitution was made only for a moral and religious people. It is wholly inadequate to the government of any other." Was he right? Is this still true? Is the tug of war on our constitution evidence that that the U.S. Constitution is inadequate for the Me-Now culture? Manifesting itself in our Me-Now culture, this separation or division from God has been, is, and will be the source of discord for seasons to come unless we find the right shepherds to lead our nation, our state, our communities, our churches, our homes, and our lives.

Not only is our nation divided against God, we are also divided against ourselves. The "moral and religious people" are not exempt. How do I know? I was divided against Him because I was focused on "Me" and "Now" and thought I was the exception to the rule. As long as I tried to do right, I was fine. I knew He had called me, but I was divided like we are now in the government chambers, in our homes, in our families, or at work. However, the greatest division is of His Church (not *in* the church). Satan has divided us since the beginning of mankind on what makes our individual belief, faith, customs—religion—different and more favorable in God's eyes. But we have managed to focus on our religion and lose sight of the important item that should unite us—the love that is in Jesus Christ. We build our own silos with our own independent thinking in places where we worship in order to make our brand of faith comfortable. We have become both Standard and New-Norm stewards at the same time because leaders conform. Do not misread me... that is not all bad, but a divisive stewardship does not lend itself to the higher calling. Focusing on the differences such as: how we believe, whether or not we use real wine in communion, how we conduct our church services, how we sing our songs, who are considered the saints, what Bible version should we use to quote scriptures, how should we hold our hands for communion, on how we say our prayers, when do we get the Holy Spirit, how should we elect our pastors, when we can walk into the church, who is saved, how do we show that we are saved, is it Holy Ghost or the Holy Spirit, who is going to hell, who has the biggest church, do we say "humble" or "umble", who has the longest/shortest sermon, who can tithe enough to have a relationship with the senior pastor, who can be buried in the church, what's the right number of church services, and even on who can serve keeps us from being perfect harmony. That's a big list; but you've likely encountered one or more of these issues in your church. With all our infighting, it is no wonder we have gaps in the walls, it is no wonder we have chaos and judgment, no wonder the Me-Now culture is consuming what is sacred, no wonder less people are going to worship, and it is no wonder we may have more steward leaders than any other type of leader.

Nevertheless... What does Nehemiah's playbook say about how stewards are to govern and should be governed? As a first step, Nehemiah reinstituted the sharing and reading of God's word. It was important to refocus temple stewards to take proper care of the temple and the spiritual well-being of the people. With 62.5 percent of people in the U.S. not attending regular worship services, where is the Word of God coming from, where are the "experts" on the Word, who is providing expert advice, or where is the discernment coming from?

Discernment helps you recognize that leaders leading stewards can be fueled by selfishness, ambition, and jealousy. Sometimes, we only need the leader in the mirror to adhere to force others to our yearning demands. Taking people's advice just because they are called an expert,

Chapter 5: Steward Leadership

are friendly, or have status places you and those that you lead at risk. There is no substitute for knowledge of the Word of God. Do you fear the powerful elite in your community, accept perceived inadequacies, and succumb as a humble steward? There is nothing wrong with accepting that steward or humble servant role if we are honoring and glorifying God. The problem arises when that stewardship is in honor of man, a principle, a narrative, a utility, a group, or an earthly desire. The leader in the mirror needs discernment not to succumb to those things. Why? The Word of God is how we discern and detect error. There will be many voices that compete for our attention and focus—our called purpose. We all should expect to hear from Him and we need to test this for ourselves. However, if the leader in the mirror does not have discernment, surround yourself with people who do; who are stewards of the Word of God and not of man.

Chapter 6:
GATEKEEPER LEADERSHIP

CUE LEADERSHIP MATRIX©

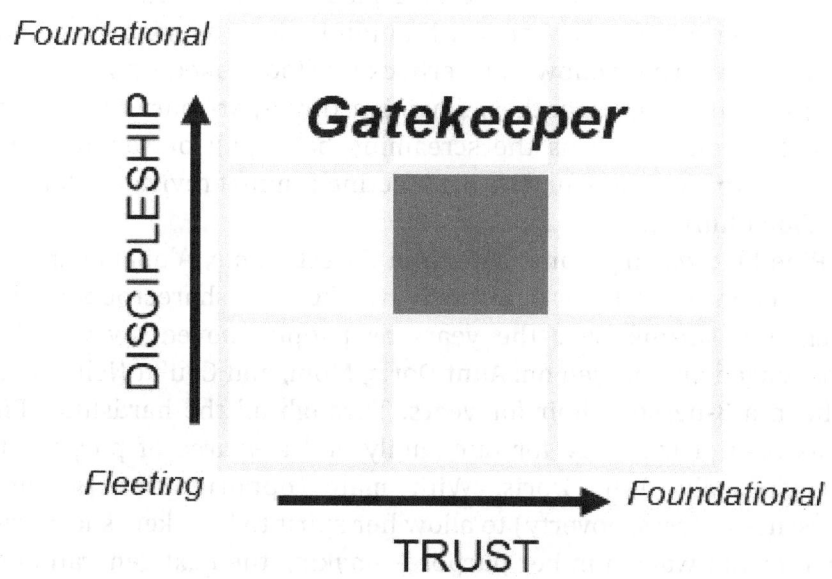

"Uncle Bay ain't gonna kill me!"
—Fox Boys

As I shared in chapter 4, I stopped speaking when I was about 4 years old and did not speak many words until after age 5. No one knew of the trauma I had experienced, and what I am told was that I just pointed at things. (At times now, I am sure my family wishes that was still the case.) I was a shy kid, and Jody was one of the few who could get me to talk. Mom surely could, as well as Mom's sister, my Aunt Doris Peagler. Mom and Aunt Doris are a lot alike but they do have some stark differences. They both operate from a biblical view and seek to serve others first. Mom, the older, is more pleasing and docile, while Aunt

Chapter 6: Gatekeeper Leadership

Doris is more direct and forceful. They work well together in life, in church, and on us. Aunt Doris' persistence was no match for any wall or obstacle. She has a drive like no other, and no chasm was too large for her to tackle, even my shyness, fear, or unwillingness to engage. Aunt Doris put me in situations where I had to come out of my shell. She fostered my development and helped me to find my voice again. How? Along with Mom, they threw me in a place where I found myself in carrying the crown for the Lomaxx-Hannon Junior College homecoming queen while wearing yellow knickerbockers (Jody joked on me for two weeks); reading short speeches; singing a three-part harmony (mostly Jody, with Donna and I as the screaming backups); or saying poems during Christmas, Easter, or The Big Meeting (annual revival at Pine Flat A.M.E. Zion Church).

Pine Flat was my home church in Forest Home, Alabama and sits on the plantation where our family worked as sharecroppers. Our congregation shrunk over the years as people moved away and as members aged and passed on. Aunt Doris, Mom, and Cou'nt Nellie Smith have been a 3-person choir for years. Through all the hardships, Pine Flat has been a mainstay for our family and a source of purpose for many, especially Aunt Doris. With many opportunities (sickness, heartlessness, stress, poverty) to allow her spirit to be taken, she carried the mantle and walked in her purpose—making the next generation for the better... a true servant.

Aunt Doris could tell the best stories. After my grandfather Hugh Mack (her father), Aunt Doris is the best storyteller I know. She was also the best negotiator. Simply, she had an art for persuasion. When she asked you to do something, there was only one answer, and it had to be quick. It really was never an "ask" but rather a directive. Aunt Doris usually wanted me (us before Donna and Jody went off to college) to be on the program at church on Sunday or a function on Saturday. That meant that I was to read the responsive reading, say a prayer, open the program with a welcome, or participate in a youth group function. The only excuse I had not to go if she put me on the program was for a school-related function... math tournament, track meet, etc. One Saturday, I was caught off-guard. After a late Friday night (in which I was out with friends), Mom shared that Aunt Doris had put me on program the next morning. There was this get-together that everyone was going to. I wanted to go hang out at the big barbeque/fish fry/picnic one of the fellas was having. Choosing between church on Saturday or a picnic on Saturday, the choice was obvious to me. I was *not* on program...

I boldly woke up that Saturday morning with the intent to go to the picnic and called Aunt Doris on the phone. I told her that I could not make it. She asked if I had a math tournament or something, and I told her no. She asked, "Then, what's the problem?" I said that I had plans. "Plus," I added, "You did not ask me." As soon as the words exited my mouth, I knew I had messed up. There was silence on the phone and a warm sensation on the back of my neck. The warm sensation was Mom's stare because I'd sassed a grown-up, not just any grown-up, but her sister. After a few seconds, Aunt Doris asked, "Have I ever refused anything you have asked me to do?" As I was about to answer, she cut me off and said, "Don't answer. Let me talk to your momma." As Mom took the phone, she said in a matter-of-fact way, "Don't worry. If he does not come to your program, he will not leave the house today." She looked at me with a serious look as she said it. Well, I guess I was on program after all. Mom caught me off guard. Once I got there, I just hugged Aunt Doris and asked for forgiveness. She simply said, "Be consistent and don't catch people that depend on you off-guard by leaving them hanging."

Speaking of getting caught off-guard, Tai and I were caught off-guard by the difference in personalities between our two daughters. Lovingly, one is a butterfly who seeks to comply, and one is honey badger who seeks to defy... Mom and Aunt Doris, respectively. I should have known it would be that way, considering all the different personalities among my own siblings. We all have similarities, but also stark differences. Sheila (Shee-Bug) was the responsible, the resilient, and the tenacious one. Shari (Shoo) had uncommon fight, focus, and persistence where she either loved you or hated you, with no in-between. Tom (TP) was the Boy Scout who was always dependable and hard working. Gladys (Scarlett) was the dreamer, matched with loving and passionate spirit. If you mold caring, toughness, skepticism, and loyalty in one person, that one person would be Patricia (Patty Baby). Donna (B) had to have all the attention, as well as all command and control of her situations. Ronald (Jody), full of fun and adventure, took risks and was a rebel. Then there was me, hard-headed and full of

Chapter 6: Gatekeeper Leadership

questions. All of us can be prideful and bull-headed. Why was I surprised at Kennedy and Karson? How did Mom and Dad manage all these needs, personalities, and differences? They just did. They didn't love any of us more or less than the others, but handled us differently according to our different response languages. Even today, Mom can tell by the tone of my voice if something is wrong.

One day our teacher, the great Mrs. Ruby Womack, told Mom, "Let me tell you the differences in your sons. If you ask Tom to do something, he will do it with no questions. If you asked Jody to do something, he just won't do it at all. If you ask Eric to do something, he will ask why and will do it his way." Mrs. Womack knew us well. I said "our teacher" because she was not only the teacher for my sisters and brothers, but she taught my mom as young teacher decades before. That is a legacy. She stood apost for over 30 years across multiple generations.

Mrs. Ruby Womack was the sweetest but toughest teacher you could imagine. She knew how to balance love and discipline and knew how to challenge us. She was spot on with her assessment and taught me one of my first lessons on leadership during a social studies project. She would often break us up in teams for project work. One person would lead, plan, assign roles, and facilitate the completion. Regardless if I was officially assigned as leader or not, the work seemed to give birth to one person's vision—mine. On this particular project, she purposely placed me as the leader. She observed as she always did. I guess she noticed during the planning session that I was not taking input from the team. I rejected everything: ideas, advice, color schemes, verbiage, and even the paper choice that the rest of the team came up with. I had a vision of what this project on the State of Illinois was going to be. No one was going to get in my way. I had focused discipline about the Land of Lincoln. One day, she encouraged (warned) me to not to take over the project and to let everyone else have input. I appeased the team by giving them the glamorous roles of holding the posters and props and of introducing me as the speaker. Even that was risky, but I could not allow my team to disrupt my vision. This was pure manipulation. Then, the big day came. No one on earth knew more than me about Illinois... My team held the posters and props. I received a great introduction and spoke like Lincoln did when he announced his candidacy for the President of the United States. Then, the grade came. My team received a

95 as a grade, and I personally received a measly 75. What! Mrs. Womack shocked me. When I asked her about it, she simply asked if me if I "blocked and ran the football at the same time."

I got the message, and she taught me a lesson on leading people—engaging, placing the team first, and being accountable to them. Plus, teamwork was worth 15 points on the project. Who knew? I would have if I was not so engulfed in myself. Her assessment of Tom and Sarah's three boys was right.

She also taught three other boys—the Fox Boys. William, Bobby, and Steve were the youngest of my Aunt Gladys Fox's seven children. These three cousins were true keepers of the gate when it came to Jody and me. They grew up with a single mother in our extended family. Collectively, they were a wealth of knowledge, perspectives, fun, and mentorship. However, for some reason, whenever they were about to do something (with or without permission), Bobby and Steve would allow Jody to go along but not me. Jody was a little closer to them in age. "Uncle Bay ain't gonna kill me!" was the favorite line my cousins used that stopped all my pleading to follow them. They loved and respected their Uncle Bay, my dad. Dad served as a father figure for them as well as many others. Auntie Fox used to call down the road to our house for Dad to come get her boys in line. They got in line, for they knew, just like we all knew, that Dad did not bluff when it came to discipline.

Outside of their heavily starched jeans, white hi-top Chuck Taylors, and Kangol caps, what I loved the most about the Fox Boys was the competition and the philosophical conversation. Leaving a huddle session with Fox Boys either we were laughing, enlightened, scolded, mellowed, or competing. Whether it was dominoes, checkers, chess, tunk, spades, or basketball, we could count on tough competition and good conversation. Both could turn into a great pastime or a disagreement, especially when it came to playing basketball. Either we played a half-court game (no more than 4 on 4) or played a game of 21. The basic rules applied, but we had to call our own fouls. Guarding against taller and bigger men, I learned how to foul and to foul well. Each of them had a different style of game.

STEVIE-BOY

Steve, "Stevie-Boy" as Auntie Fox called him, was the purest

Chapter 6: Gatekeeper Leadership

shooter I have seen. He would pull up from anywhere and hit a shot. Before there was 3-point line, he was shooting beyond that. I have seen him walk a ball down ten feet past half court and pull up a shot. He hit sometimes and missed sometimes. He was not a selfish player though. His confidence in his ability to make a basket was unmatched. His game style fit his personality—rebel, gambler, and rule breaker. Stevie-Boy would bet on anything—a shot, fishing, cards, anything where he could get odds. He had the ability to count the odds in his head mathematically quicker than most. He was tough to beat and was always in a game somewhere betting. He had game on the court, with the ladies, and in competition.

If there was one thing that Dad hated outside of drugs it was gambling of any kind. Apparently, my grandfather, Dad's Dad, was a mathematic genius, but used it to gamble. Legend had it that he could count cards better than anyone. It helped him win as well as got him in a little trouble at times. People would accuse him of cheating. I'm not sure of all the details, but I know Dad despised it. Stevie-Boy knew it, too. That didn't stop him from using his "gift." He was often the leader in trying new things, getting into mischief, or gaming a situation—from sneaking into a private pond to fish, commandeering a private pool while the owners were away, pitching to the line, or to showing us how to make and smoke cigarettes. Stevie-Boy, along with Jody and my sisters, Patricia and Donna, never wanted me come along with them. But one day, they had no choice because there no place to leave me. And it was the last time that I, or any of them, went. Instead of going to hide in the nearby woods, we decided to set up under a simple shelter behind our home. I had built the shelter by combining a few cardboard boxes and camouflaged it with weeds, branches, and kudzu. I used to use my camouflage to catch birds with a trap made from a box propped up with a stick tied to a string and with bait (bread crumbs) positioned about 15 yards away. The idea was to pull the string and entrap birds as they went after the bait under the box. I was not as successful, in retrospect, for the bird smelled my scent around the bait. Plus, they had to have seen me. Instead of using the bird blind to trap birds, we used the camouflage to hide our smoking experiments. The cigarettes were simple and made from dried dogweed plant. The smoking paper was brown paper bags. Stevie-Boy obviously was the most experienced as we passed the "joint" around.

As it moved closer to me, I watched the joint burn more unevenly and the paper get wetter. Then, it was my turn. Jody said, under his constant watch over me, "You don't have to, if you don't want to." Then, Stevie-Boy chastised, "Scared? Say, you scared?" I was trapped, just like I had imagined those birds would be. I looked around to everyone and realized that it would make everyone feel more comfortable if I did it. That is to say, I could not snitch if I took the hit. So, I took the dogweed joint and took a long drag. Wouldn't you know, I forgot to exhale, turned blue, and passed out. As I was coming back to life, I heard commotion, Donna was trying to give me month-to-mouth, Pat was crying, "We done killed him!" and Stevie-Boy was shaking me, saying "Uncle Bay is gonna kill me!" They thought I had died. Needless to say, either they never smoked again or I was not invited. That was probably the reason why Stevie-Boy never let me hang. The "dogweed" story lives in infamy. So does how Stevie-Boy used me to shift the momentum of a game. He never dared me much after that, but he used me to game a few folks. From betting a kids five plus years older to footrace "lil ol" me, Stevie-Boy went as far as to give one older kid a head start. Every time, I'd catch him or her, pass, and stretch the lead. This may sound questionable, but realize the amount confidence that he showed and built in the smallest person in our community. From going for the steal on the basketball court, to leading with a spade when playing cards, or sprinting down the court on every rebound (he would toss it to me for an easy layup because I outran everyone), he placed building blocks for a small, shy, passive kid.

BOBBY JOE

And then there was Bobby, "Bobby Joe." Bobby Joe was the next youngest Fox Boy, two years older than Stevie-Boy. Bobby Joe had this indescribable discipline and focus whether he was reading, wrestling, working... and especially shooting a basketball. He did not have the range that Stevie-Boy had, but from 18-feet or less from the basket, Bobby Joe rarely missed. He could also run a clinic on hustling. He knew how to position himself for rebounds, and score more "garbage" points than anyone in the history of Mt. Zion. When we played a game of 21, a player could come off the free throw line and have a free shot after

Chapter 6: Gatekeeper Leadership

hitting 3 free throws in a row. If Bobby Joe managed to hit that first free shot, he would usually win the game, even when we guarded him. There were times in a game when no one else besides Bobby Joe got a chance to take a shot because Bobby would not miss a free throw. He would rook us with hustle, garbage points, and unwavering disciplined free throws. He has such a quick release on his shot where we had to be ready to defend as soon as he touched the ball. Even when we defended him, he forced and made impossible shots... He was a machine with no off switch.

As I reflect on it, it was amazing to see. But he would only rook us every so often because we would foul him with bad intentions. Bobby Joe's discipline and focus was something to aspire to. We were not always on the receiving end of that discipline and hustle. When Bobby Joe, Stevie-Boy, Jody, and I played together, we believed that we could beat anyone around the way. I used to hear from Bobby Joe, "Sho't Dog, don't let him breathe!" when he wanted me to add unrelenting pressure to the point guard on the opposing team (There were no referees). Whatever he put his mind to, Bobby Joe could accomplish—good or bad. He was always all-in, all-or-nothing, and down for whatever; for a game, a fight, a lesson, or love. He had the inability to give less than all of himself. If he committed, Bobby Joe committed with an unyielding discipline.

Bobby Joe was a disciplined teacher for Jody and I, forcing us to confront realities of life—our heritage from the plantation, the importance for us to do better than the last generation, and the importance of Pops, his Uncle Bay, as a father-figure. Bobby Joe helped me and Jody understand Dad and his generation of men. During adolescence, I struggled with understanding Pops, the provider and disciplinarian, while yearning for more time and affection than Pops had learned to give to his sons. All of Fox's boys, especially Bobby Joe, knew how to appeal to me or question my logic. He would always say that I should be glad I had my father in my life and I should be glad he was home every night because, Bobby Joe would say, "I don't know where mine is." When I was around 14 years old, he knew that I was studying Mark Twain and used a famous quote from Twain to let me know that I did *not* know it all. Bobby did not know the quote verbatim, but he shared, "When I was a boy of 14, my father was so ignorant I could hardly stand to have the old man around. But when I got to be 21, I was astonished at how much the old man had learned in seven years."

Of course, the point was that Twain's father was not the one that had learned anything in the seven-year period. That quote helped me and served me mightily. I did not waste any more time trying to understand but decided to just love my Pops. Although I admired Bobby Joe for his discipline and hustle, I had not realized that he had learned it from Pops.

My dad lost his battle with cancer on Good Friday 2013, and I thank Bobby Joe for opening my eyes. I have no regrets, for I received more than what I yearned for from Pops. Bobby Joe was all in, committed, and tenacious, whether it was teaching me the pick-and-roll or sharing the importance of having a man like my dad in my life. I learned from the discipline of Bobby Joe in so many ways, even though he could not maintain discipline in his own life at times. Never healing from the death of Auntie Fox or his older brother William, Bobby Joe suffered much. One thing never has changed for Bobby Joe—his all-in, committed, and tenacious love of family.

POO-BEAR

William, "Poo-Bear," loved to back his opponent down, turn, and fade away with a high-arching jump shot—pre-Jordan. He'd be running his mouth the entire time, but always with a smile. Once he made the shot, he told the defender what he did wrong or why he was able to make the shot. Poo-Bear took the opening the defender gave and exploited it. He was a teacher of sorts, but not the kind that coddled a student. Poo-Bear did not play as much as others because of his bad knees (or so he said). But his gait gave him a natural "pimp walk." Most brothers had to fake it, but Poo-Bear had it naturally. He was always freshly manicured and did not want to mess up his white Chuck Taylors (That's my theory of why he did not play much). Normally, you could find him on watch over kids and the elderly in the neighborhood. Anyone that did not belong or who was up to no good, he would confront, ask questions, and even run them out of the community. One day, he went as far as to run the county commissioner candidate out of the neighborhood because we only saw him during campaign season. Always looking to teach, Poo-Bear chastised him, accusing him of

Chapter 6: Gatekeeper Leadership

looking to prey on people who fall victim to their circumstances and Poo-Bear told me that I better "never let anyone tell you how to vote." Meeting and talking with Poo-Bear, one would not have guessed that he was an ex-con. He could talk on range of topics—from subject-verb agreement to quantum physics or from Socrates to pluralism.

He was a leader who made a humongous mistake from which he never quite recovered. Home on military leave, he and some friends robbed a local country convenience store. I do not know how it all went down, but Poo-Bear was the only one who went to prison. Poo-Bear and I had a special relationship—open, honest, and shocking. I asked him one day what happened in the store. He admitted having the gun for a period of time. In fact, the gun was not his and was not even loaded, but he held it while the others took the money. I asked him, "How stupid was that?" He admitted that he was stupid, that the event changed his life, and that he lost a promising career in the Marines. Poo-Bear had an extremely high IQ and tested off the charts in high school and in the military. He was a ferocious reader and was often underestimated because of his past. He passed his time in prison by reading. Essentially, Poo-Bear became one of the neighborhood tutors, which was the source of our conflict. He wanted to help me with my studies, but I did not need his help. Even if I did, in my arrogance and pride I would not have asked. I did what I always did, figured it out on my own. He hated that and always looked for ways to engage me. He would ask what I was studying, reading that six weeks, or about "practical applications for parabolas."

One day, he took a stand on me. After getting off the bus, I undressed quickly and ran up the road behind my Aunt Fox's house to play basketball. Poo-Bear was always set up on side of her house that faced our house. He had a view of most of the neighborhood as well as the dirt basketball court behind my aunt's house. As I got closer, we greeted each other, and then he asked it, "Sho't Dawg, have you done yo'r homework?" I was shocked initially because I was thinking about the nerve he had for asking *me*, a straight A student, if I had done my homework. I did not answer the first time because I did not *have* to answer. I didn't need his help.

He asked again, and I replied, "What?"

He stood up off the bench and said in a louder voice, "You heard me, lil n****. Have you done your homework?"

I boldly said, "No! I have not. What's it to ya?"

Poo-Bear said, "If you don't get yo' *** back down that road and do yo' homework, I'm gonna kick yo' lil ********ing, ***!" (Poo-Bear's words were raw. I'm keeping his phraseology so you can get the full flavor of these interactions. And, although I do not use it now, it wasn't anything for us to use the racial slur dubbed "the 'n' word" on each other at that time.)

By that time, in his limped walk, he got right in my face, looking down at me and blocking my path. Then he said, "You ain't playing today until you finished you homework!"

I asked him confidently, "What is yo' problem today?" I felt no sense of threat from him, but I was confused by his posturing. Plus he did not have moonshine on his breath. He was sober but serious.

Poo-Bear said, "If you don't get yo' *** back down the road and do your homework, I gonna kick your *** and then I gonna tell Uncle Bay so he can kick yo' *** for not doing it and for disrespecting your elders!"

I replied with disgust, "Fool, you ain't no elder! Get out of my way before I mess up your white jeans and your Chuck Taylors!"

I tried walking around him, but he was serious. He said, "You gonna have to fight me to play today!" By this time the whole neighborhood was watching. I knew if I did not go and do my homework, I would have to fight him. Then he said, "I gonna be here every day checking to see if you have done your homework, keeping the gate to this court and to this ball. Everybody else can come, but yo' entry is your homework!"

I decided to back down and not make a bigger scene. I was not scared, but I knew he was more serious than usual. Explaining a tussle with my beloved cousin to Mom and Dad was not what I wanted. As I turned away, he shoved the back of my right shoulder and boldly said, "I thought so." I let him punk me. I thought I would walk down, wait a little while, and come back because I only had to read anyway. He wouldn't know the difference. Poo-Bear asked me what I had for homework.

I said, "You wouldn't know about it anyway!"

He sharply answered, "Try me, fool!"

I told him that I had to read the beginning of Act II of *Macbeth*. Then it happened. He shook me, shocked me, and showed me something. He said, "OK. When you come back, I want you to tell me how

Chapter 6: Gatekeeper Leadership

Macbeth's dagger scene applies to me, past or present." I would not give him the satisfaction of knowing I was shocked by what he asked, for. Poo-Bear was deep. He squashed my plans not to read. In fact, he changed the dynamics of our relationship that day in so many ways. This scene he referred to was probably the most important scene in terms of plot and character development in *Macbeth*. When Macbeth hallucinated the dagger, the dagger symbolized Macbeth's guilt and fear. At that moment, Macbeth is at a crossroads and had to decide on which path to travel. He was questioning and challenging his fate while searching for the right decision.

Just like Macbeth, Poo-Bear had been at many crossroads too many times in life and did not want me to feel the fear, uncertainty, or guilt that he was feeling then. He knew that life was a collection of choices and wanted me to choose wisely. Instead of hallucinating, he drowned himself in Ray-Hard bootleg whiskey. Ray-Hard was a legendary moonshiner from a nearby community called Pigeon Creek. The rumor had it that the liquor he sold had been in the ground for 7 years. He even had a red-tint shine that he cured in oak barrels. Although it would eat through a styrofoam cup, Ray-Hard was so smooth that it was easy to drink too much of it. Ray-Hard did not burn going down your throat. The shine was quality, cheap, and accessible, costing only $20 a gallon. It could last a month or more if you had one drinking buddy, but with three or more drinking buddies, a gallon of Ray-Hard may not last a day. Poo-Bear drank so much Ray-Hard, the moonshine was a part of him mentally, physically, and spiritually. Seeping out of his pores was the smell of Ray-Hard. He only needed a match, and he would go up in flames or explode as he did on me that day. He had tried every nice way to get involved in my choices, until he took that stand that day and forced himself into my world.

From that day on, we spoke philosophy; from Socrates to Alexander the Great, from Machiavelli to John Locke, from MLK to Malcolm X. He consumed books, Ray-Hard, and good music. Poo-Bear would listen to any artist with a special craft, with a message, or certain philosophy. He liked the black rock (funk and metal) band Living Color, led by Corey Glover. His favorite, as well as was true for all of the Powell boys, was Bob Marley. Marley inspired a movement on freedom that connected with spirits of oppressed people. Marley's lyrics seemed to put him in a trance at times. Poo-Bear was so serious about Marley that he tried to assign me a paper to write on his favorite song—"Redemption Song." That day, he and Bobby Joe called me up the road to sit and listen to music. He said, "Listen to the greatest song ever written." I said in a smart-alecky tone, "I have heard this song before." Then Poo-Bear replied, "But you have not *really* heard it." He stopped the cassette tape, rewound, and hit play. "Listen," he said, "this is the most profound verse in all of music."

I remember thinking, "There he goes with his philosophizing." Then the verse came. Marley sang, "Have no fear for atomic energy, 'cause none of them can stop the time."

William asked, "What does this mean to you?"

I was still contemplating because I had not stopped and "really heard" it. Bobby Joe asked me to think about recent history. "Cold war with Russia," he said. I could tell that these brothers had thought this through. They were testing, but not teasing, and were trying to give me a piece of them. Poo-Bear said, "No matter how much we humans think of ourselves with our power and weapons, we cannot stop the time. Not even a nuclear weapon can stop it." Then he said, "Man cannot destroy that which he did not have a hand in making."

What he meant was that God created all of this, and we are shallow to think that we could muster enough destruction to destroy His creation. So he said in a loving and earnest tone, "Sho't Dawg, don't let fear consume you. Don't make decisions out of fear. And don't let someone p*** on your head and tell you it's raining. You ain't no Joe Poole n**** like me. You are smarter than that. You are the best of us. Don't disappoint! No fear in this game or in life! You are a lion from Zion!" I was speechless, but had a chuckle inside thinking, "*Joe Poole n****?* Where does he come up with this stuff...?"

I realized through his shocking words even more that the Fox Boys loved me. They knew what I dealing with at the time. I was just about to follow in the largest set of footprints in my world... those left by my brother Jody as the starting quarterback of the Greenville High Tigers and by my brother Tom, who was legendary in the community, city, and state. The word around town and in the community was that I too small and would not be like them, regardless of my speed.

From that day forward, Bob Marley became my homework and

Chapter 6: Gatekeeper Leadership

study partner and fear of failure or fear of trying something new loosened its noose. I had to use that fearlessness much in life but had to use it a few months later on Poo-Bear himself. His fuse was lit one day when one of my best friends dropped me off after a baseball game. Matt "Chapel" Shepherd was and remains a dear friend, and he and I hung out all the time. As Matt got out of the car greeting and laughing with Dad, I raised my hand toward my Auntie Fox's house to speak to Poo-Bear. Before I could get my hand half way in the air, Poo-Bear was half way down the hill walking with his fast limp. I had seen that walk before, and it smelled of trouble. I was right because Poo-Bear screamed out, "White Boy! Hey White Boy! What in the h*** you doing down here? You hear me White Boy?" Matt, who was white, looked at me and asked calmly, "What's his problem?" This did not surprise Matt because Matt was as tough as they came. Plus, he knew that we would not let anything happen to him. I said to Matt, "Nothing will happen. Whatever you do, do not let him punk you. Just be yourself, do not act scared or overly confident." As Poo-Bear entered our yard, he darted to Matt and said, "White Boy, White Boy, you heard me calling you. It is time for you to get your *** out from down here!" At this point, Poo-Bear and Matt were standing nose to nose. Matt said, "My name aint 'White Boy.' Plus, the last time I checked, this was Mr. Tommie's and Ms. Sarah's yard."

Poo-Bear said, "I speak for my uncle here."

Dad said promptly and quickly, "Ain't nobody speak for me. Leave that boy alone."

Poo-Bear threatened again, "If you don't leave, I'm gonna kick yo' white *** all the way where you came from. Every time I catch you down here, I'm gonna kick yo' ***."

Then Matt said the greatest line ever, "Then we gonna be two ***-kicking mutha***** today!" Then, Matt looked quickly at Dad and said, "Excuse me Mr. Tommie." They stared each other down for another 30 seconds without either of them blinking an eye. Then Poo-Bear smiled and said, "I like you white boy. You ain't scared of nothin'. Are you?" He looked at me and said, "Sho't Dawg, he can hang with you. He will have yo' back! No doubt." He looked at Matt and said, "I luv me some White Boy. What's your name? Who your people?"

From that point on, Poo-Bear rooted for Matt and embraced him like a brother. Dad and I knew that he would not harm Matt, but (I guess) it was Poo-Bear's way of protecting me, knowing that "Jim Crow" still lurked around our city. Poo-Bear also knew that people in our small town did not take too kindly of white and black hanging out like Matt and I did. If Matt had punked out and not stood his ground, I would have heard it from Poo-Bear every day, asking why I hang with this "soft dude."

I was just glad that Poo-Bear did not try to slap him. Slapping was Poo-Bear's signature. When he had a little too much Ray-Hard, he had a tendency to slap people. He slapped me once. I forget what we were doing but it was his last time. I body-slammed him hard and dragged him across the grass. The body slam was enough to make my point, but I wanted to mess up his freshly starched white jeans. The grass stain on the left leg never came out. I gave a smirk every time he wore them. I had to use that fearlessness a few years later on Poo-Bear again. We were at a family reunion in Mt. Zion, the first one after Auntie Fox lost her battle with cancer. Poo-Bear and Ray-Hard were intimate that day. He was what we called "lit up." He had stumbled a few times throughout the day. Without anyone knowing, he decided that it was time to leave because he had to go home and sleep before taking his shift that night at work. I heard his sister Shirley say that she wished that someone would drive him home, and then suddenly, we heard a crash. Poo-Bear backed his car into Tom's SUV and then had the audacity to scream out the window, "Tom Barkley, come move yo' **** car!"

At that point, most of the men of the family rushed to the scene trying to convince Poo-Bear to give up his keys. Poo-Bear got irate; he started swearing and pushing people. No one was going to get those keys without upsetting our family gathering. So, I walked up calmly thinking that if anyone could get the keys from him, I could. I asked for the keys, and he told me in select language what we could all do with ourselves. Without thinking, I shocked him by giving him some of his own medicine. I slapped his face, took the keys out of his tight hands, swirled him around to face the car, grabbed the back of his collar like he was a puppy, marched him around to the back of the car, opened the front passenger door, tossed him into the car, and shut the door on him. I did all this without saying a word, and did it so fast that he never realized what hit him until he was in the passenger seat of his car. My move was desperate, but it was classic of what Poo-Bear himself would

Chapter 6: Gatekeeper Leadership

do. I had not drank any alcohol because Tai and I had to drive back to college that evening. I drove him home and was protecting him. He did not say a word during the entire 30-mile trip to the other side of the county. He did not fall asleep at all as I had expected. I think the slap and quick moves may have sobered him. Before he got out of the car, the 'oracle of Zion' finally spoke. He said in a sobered voice, "Sho't Dawg, now you know that you are the only person in the world that could have done that and gotten away with it."

I said in joking and sarcastic way, "Don't mention it."

Then he said, "Don't let that **** happen again."

I laughed and asked, "Does the little baby need help in the house?" He just glared at me and got out of the car.

The ironic thing is that he kept the gate, in spite of being weighed down by his own personal philosophies on life. As with Bobby Joe who was "down-for-whatever," he would force an event by any means necessary with unwavering discipline. Or like Stevie-Boy who would bet on himself, taking risks without understanding the outcomes or based on feeling. Or as Poo-Bear who would slap almost anyone, he would test you for reaction and game you into doing exactly what he wanted. Knowingly or not, they survived on these philosophies. Looking back, those same philosophies manifested in me. They worked at times but weighed me down more often than I realized—from having an unwavering focus on saving a failing business to taking risks on a job or to shocking and manipulating the ladies with a persona that always had an agenda. With me and with them, our philosophical approach was marred with seeking survival, significance, self-preservation, self-worth, self-esteem, significance, status, and an agenda.

The love, adventure, philosophies, and the pain of the Fox Boys built a fence around us. These brothers impressed upon me to always have facts, to have the right questions when I did not have the facts, and to be fearless with my perspectives and God-given talents. These beloved brothers stood apost. Sadly, Poo-Bear died in a car accident when he fell asleep doped up on flu medication. He never had children, but a piece of him lives in me, just as a piece of Pops lived in them. They protected us, schooled us, and enlightened us about social, educational, economic, and political parts of our Societal Ecosystem… about life. For many seasons, they were Gatekeepers.

Gatekeepers are people who are given a system and taught to govern its sphere of influence or talents. They look to improve or optimize their sphere of influence or domain. Pops put the Fox Boys in charge and held them responsible not only for us but for the Village. Fox Boys revered Pops and stood apost daily in joy... not in grief or burden. If they did that for Pops, how much more can the leader in mirror do while anchored in, in awe of, or in reverence to God?

In Isaiah 62:6-7 we read: "I have posted watchmen on your walls, Jerusalem; they will never be silent day or night. You who called on the Lord, give yourselves no rest, and give him no rest until he establishes Jerusalem and makes her the praise of the earth."

The Lord assigns watchmen. Have you been set in place as a watchman (or watchwoman)? Are there people around you whom you need to equip and appoint as watchmen? Nehemiah knew the importance of the watchman role well. He put his brother Hanani along with Hanniah, commander of the citadel, in charge of Jerusalem after the walls had been rebuilt. Nehemiah chose Hannaiah because Hannaiah feared God more than most men did. They kept watch at the gates and prepared more gatekeepers like Akkub, Talmon, and their 170 associates (Ne 11:19) to stand apost to guard the walls, homes, businesses, what was sacred, and what God had rebuilt. When true transformational change happens, we need gatekeepers keep to watch, to secure the gate and to secure future of the vision. If these gatekeepers falter, the transformational leader (the shepherd) has to come back to wield influence, or else the change falters. Nehemiah had to come back to set the people back on course. In corporate America, we call them "effective leaders"—they assess, inspire action, are optimistic, have integrity, engage teams, are confident, communicate, and are decisive. Imagine that type of leader anchored in the Lord. In corporate transformations, we assign "champions" around initiatives. In either case, leadership could fail to choose or raise the right champion who is trusted, liked, and respected; fail to inspire or identify the unsung leaders to come forward and take the mantle; fail to anoint a champion with authority to make decisions and hold others accountable; fail to equip with resources and protection to accomplish the mission. Despite initial successes, failure to provide sustained and coordinated leadership leads to gaps in the walls and cracks in the gate. There will be

Chapter 6: Gatekeeper Leadership

rapid performance slippage, erosion of early gains, and certain irrelevance of the initiative or effort. If this gap exists in society, we shouldn't fool ourselves that the gaps do not exist in companies.

We have seen the same thing time and time again in history where the gates are reopened, cracked, or flooded. There were not true gatekeepers after Lincoln's death to continue his vision. No gatekeeper took up the hat, and this nation suffered through another century of hardened hearts from those with influence and power.

The ill-equipped leaders that took, ceased, or hoarded the proverbial baton from Dr. King's death were certainly no drum majors and were not gatekeepers of loving, surrendering, healing, or joining hands in that "ol' Negro Spiritual." No gatekeeper took up the baton there either, and this nation is suffering through another half-century of hard hearts—Ferguson, Missouri is only symptomatic of it. In both cases, we had a death of a shepherd, a gap filler, a messenger, as well as the death of a transformation in a public forum. Leaders with hardened hearts filled the gap and built mounds of unsustainable armistice.

Today we (the Me-Now culture) are trying to bring about the death of God and bring about the death of the name of "Jesus" in the public forum (schools, events, national day of prayer, etc.) because it "offends" people. We need gatekeepers to stand apost, for it was Christ Himself who told us to do so. Jesus warned of this in Mark 13:33-37, when He said, "Be on guard! Be alert! You do not know when that time will come. It's like a man going away: He leaves his house and puts his servants in charge, each with his assigned task, and tells the one at the door to keep watch. Therefore keep watch because you do not know when the owner of the house will come back... If he comes suddenly, do not let him find you sleeping. What I say to you, I say to everyone: 'Watch!'" We need to raise and anoint gatekeepers to stand apost in the gap wearing the full armor of God, as the Apostle Paul shared in Ephesians 6:10-18:

> 10 Finally, be strong in the Lord and in his mighty power. 11 Put on the full armor of God, so that you can take your stand against the devil's schemes. 12 For our struggle is not against flesh and blood, but against the rulers, against the authorities, against the powers of this dark world and against the spiritual forces of evil in the heavenly realms. 13

> Therefore put on the full armor of God, so that when the day of evil comes, you may be able to stand your ground, and after you have done everything, to stand. 14 Stand firm then, with the belt of truth buckled around your waist, with the breastplate of righteousness in place, 15 and with your feet fitted with the readiness that comes from the gospel of peace. 16 In addition to all this, take up the shield of faith, with which you can extinguish all the flaming arrows of the evil one. 17 Take the helmet of salvation and the sword of the Spirit, which is the word of God. 18 And pray in the Spirit on all occasions with all kinds of prayers and requests. With this in mind, be alert and always keep on praying for all the Lord's people.

We need to you look at the leader in the mirror to self-assess... check your armor. Yes, the leader in the mirror can ask if he or she inspires action, is optimistic, has integrity, engages the team, is confident, communicates, and is decisive. However, more importantly ask yourself... What is your integrity molded by? Do you have discernment? Are you constrained by your own philosophy? Do you serve others before serving self? Are you equally as persistent as your challenges? Are you guided by gamesmanship? Are you under God's favor? Are you being strong in the Lord and in His mighty power? Are you keeping the gate?

Chapter 7: TRANSFORMATIVE LEADERSHIP

CUE LEADERSHIP MATRIX©

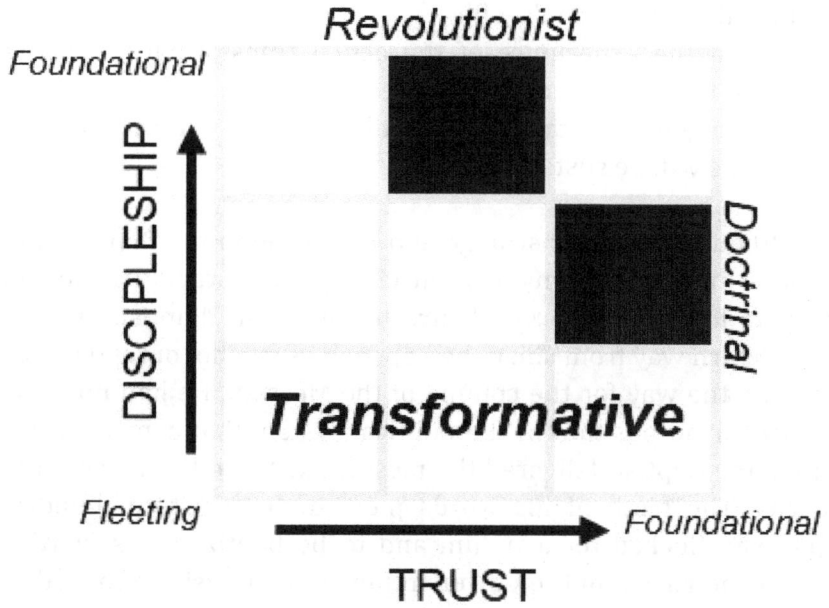

"So what?"
—Dr. Gerald Turner

What do John the Baptist, Frederick Douglass, Moses, Barbara Jordan, Stephen Biko, Robert F. Kennedy, Vernon Johns, Ezra, Eleanor Roosevelt, Jim Cates, and Dr. Gerald Turner have in common? They were and are transformative, they set the foundation for sustainable change, they began to transform the landscape of a situation, and they set the path for a transformational leader or transformational situations.

Chapter 7: Transformative Leadership

Each of these:
- Chose to love God and others first and surrendered his/her efforts as part of a designed purpose (denied self and accepted their calling);
- Led change based on a purposeful doctrine and revolutionary plan;
- Stood as a Gatekeeper with a vision of the present and a future that aligns with God's will;
- Missed the experience of the actual transformation or the end result by design or disobedience; or
- Challenged the status quo while leading—indications that the change will be sustained.

Although tagged as strange and radical, John the Baptist knew his mission in life. Unlike many of us, he clearly understood that God had set him apart for a purpose. God directed John the Baptist to challenge people to turn way from sin, to be baptized as symbol of repentance, and to prepare the way for the coming of the Messiah. He had no power, no influence, or no position in the political system that controlled his day, but John the Baptist delivered the message with God's power, force, and authority. The truth of his words pierced the hearts of hundreds of people who flocked to hear him and to be baptized. His words were anointed and gave him the power, influence, and position to lead people of his day. John the Baptist could have used his words to gain great earthly power, to win influence over the political system, and to create a revolution that was not of God but of himself. Thankfully, he never lost sight of his purpose, his calling, his mission—to point people to Jesus Christ, the Messiah.

John the Baptist did not journey to be different, to be unique, or to gain praise from everyone else but rather journeyed to be obedient, even at the risk of losing his own life. John the Baptist not only laid the path with the message but helped to build the resume for Jesus. Starting in the womb, John confirmed to his mother, Elizabeth, what the Lord had spoken to her, as John leaped in her womb (Luke 1:41-45). *Filled with the Holy Spirit, Elizabeth cried out with a loud voice and said, "Blessed are you among women, and blessed is the fruit of your womb!"*

John the Baptist shared the message about this fruit and its sweet nectar without tasting or knowing who the Messiah was until God revealed it to him. John shared that he would not have known except that God told him, *"The man on whom you see the Spirit come down and remain is he who will baptize with the Holy Spirit."* (Matthew 3:13-16)

John did not see this confirmation until after Jesus was baptized and He came up out of the water! It was Christ's baptism that revealed that Jesus belonged to God. We seldom know why the Lord calls us or know what is God's plan. We must have the discernment to know, the courage to confirm, and the selflessness to yield our position of power, authority, and influence for the ultimate transformational leader—Jesus. In John 1:30-34, John the Baptist yielded the fruit of his labor to *"a Man who has a higher rank than I."* Then John shared Jesus' resume by saying, *"for he existed before me. I did not recognize Him, but so that He might be manifested to Israel, I came baptizing in water."* Then John testified with the glowing but yielding recommendation, *"I have seen the Spirit descending as a dove out of heaven, and He remained upon Him, 'He upon whom you see the Spirit descending and remaining upon Him, this is the One who baptizes in the Holy Spirit.' I myself have seen, and have testified that this is the Son of God."*

John the Baptist was not easily impressed, for he scolded sins of the people, Pharisees, and King Herold alike. John had an unshakable vigor for the Lord. We see that same unshakable vigor in defense of the things that are not of God. Imagine that same unshakable vigor focused on transforming this Me-Now culture. Take the vigor of any group (whether seeking social rights based on a worldly definition of us; building a political narrative to maintain control by appealing to our fleshly pleasures; seeking to kill the "infidels" to gain favor on earth and in heaven; proving why a brand of religion is different, better, or pleasing to God; giving only to charities that focus on saving lives and not those focused on saving souls) and turn it for God's glory. Imagine the transformation! No, *see* the transformation that has happened, is happening, and will happen in Christ Jesus.

Jesus stayed committed to His purpose and endorsed and affirmed the transformative leader (John) that came before him, just like other Shepherds—Joshua, Shamgar, Esther as well as Nehemiah—that God called to save His people. Joshua courageously took the helm from Moses and led God's people into the Promised Land, Shamgar delivered

Chapter 7: Transformative Leadership

the people without a sword or spear (Judges 3:31), Esther became the Queen of Persia and was used by God to save His people from destruction, and Nehemiah restored God's people... he rebuilt a wall and a way of life. In his rebuilding, Nehemiah endorsed and affirmed the ministry of the transformative leader who came before him—Ezra.

Jerusalem laid in ruins, the walls were broken, the gates burned down, and the city was under constant attack by those who wanted the land and wanted to destroy its people. Before the walls could be built, the Lord had to set the proper foundation to ensure that His people would have a proper anchor. The Lord stirred Cyrus, King of Persia, to decree that the exiles could return from the land of captivity to their home in Judah (Ezra 1). In 536 B.C., the exiles made the long journey back to Jerusalem with 5,400 articles of gold and silver that had been taken from the temple seven decades earlier. The Lord sent Ezra to set the foundation... to restore worship and build the temple. For worship is the centerpiece of sustaining any nation, village, town, transformation, or home. Although resistance to the building arose and work stopped for nearly sixteen years, the foundation was set for Nehemiah as the temple was completed in 516 B.C. (Ezra 5)

Transformative leaders like Ezra set foundations for the next one to come. They seem to be before their time, like Frederick Douglass was to American Slavery. His message was not about the civil rights but about basic human rights and dignity. Douglass does not get much credit but he was an early so-called radical that our nation should have listened to more.

As the first black American elected to the Texas Senate after Reconstruction and the first southern black female elected to the United States House of Representatives, Barbara Jordan blazed the trail for many. Her ethnicity, gender, physical challenges (she had multiple sclerosis and was wheelchair-bound), background (she grew up in the hood), and health (she battled cancer and diabetes) did not stop her; she was an example for a new type of leader that does not allow life challenges to be a crutch or excuse not to try, participate, or lead. Perhaps Jordan is most known for her keynote address at the 1976 Democratic National Convention. With her booming voice she shared, "A spirit of harmony can only survive if each of us remembers, when bitterness and self-interest seem to prevail, that we share a common destiny."

She was a true difference-maker and understood that finding common ground was the foundation for leading in perfect harmony. The spirit of leading in perfect of harmony is not a new concept. A transformational leader and an instrument to end apartheid in South Africa, Nelson Mandela pursued perfect harmony, even after 27 years at Robben Island. We often forget about the one that came before Mandela, Stephen Biko. Biko was the most prominent leader who guided the movement of students' discontent into a political force that was unprecedented in the history of South Africa. Interrogated, tortured, and beaten for 22 hours by Port Elizabeth police security, Biko fell into a coma from a major head injury and was chained to a window grille for a day while in custody at the Walmer Police Station. Police loaded him in the back of a Land Rover, naked and restrained in manacles, for an 1,100 km drive to a prison hospital in Pretoria. He died shortly after arriving, and police claimed his death was the result of an extended hunger strike. Nelson Mandela said of Biko, "They had to kill him to prolong the life of apartheid."

There are others, like Robert F. Kennedy, the prelude to healers of our nation, or like Eleanor Roosevelt, another Esther, who yielded her sword of social justice in influencing her husband and other leaders of this nation. Reverend Vernon Johns, former pastor of the Ebenezer Baptist Church in Montgomery, Alabama, is considered the father of the civil rights movement. He was censored and banned because he was too radical and too truthful for the "politically correct" crowd about racism and oppression in America. The politically correct leaders of Ebenezer removed him and elected a young preacher that they were sure to control. Instead, they, we, and this nation, got a drum major, a shepherd... Dr. Martin Luther King, Jr.

I have known and experienced a few of these leaders. Jim Cates was my high school math teacher, physics teacher, math team coach, and prep bowl coach. If you picture a NASA scientist from the 60s with black rimmed glasses, side burns, and a pocket protector, you have a good idea what Mr. Cates looked like. Mr. Cates is a brilliant man, and all of his children were just as brilliant. All his kids were valedictorians of their high school class and national merit scholars. They were direct fruits of this brilliance, but I and countless of others were fruits of his brilliance

Chapter 7: Transformative Leadership

as well. He trained us to be critical thinkers, ask the right questions, and attack any problem collectively. Critical thinking was must-have skill in his classes. If you could not think critically, you would have a tough time.

Mr. Cates did not care for sports much. He used to try to convince Mom to make me stop playing sports. He would show her my grades correlated to football season or to other sports, proving that my grades were 95 and above when I was not playing sports. I understand what he was trying to do, but I believe that he did not like it that I missed his classes and math tournaments because of sports. He had a pet peeve with the school placing a monument honoring our 1987 state football championship, but not one for our state math championships. When we had to miss his class because of sports, he did not show mercy on homework or tests. He made it a policy that we take the test earlier—before school, break, or elective periods. This included all athletes—players, cheerleaders, and band members alike.

He simply cared about preparing us. Mr. Cates stretched our thinking and brought out the consultant, scientist, the problem solver in all of us. He did it with real world experiences and applications. To this day, I remember some of his real world applications. Every time I exit ramp of Interstate 85 to Interstate 65 in Montgomery, I remember one project that bothered him. We were studying banked turns in physics... finding the recommended speed for a car going around a curve. He shared a story in which he consulted with a civil engineering firm, who was designing this particular exit. He argued that the curve was designed with too much of an acute angle, requiring too low of a speed... 35 mph. He argued that it was not practical for a car to reduce its speed so low to exit and then be expected to double the speed immediately following to enter the oncoming traffic of the interstate safely. He wanted the exit to be designed with a larger radius or angled with a slight back, allowing for more speed. He did not get his way, but it was that practicality and those real life examples at every lesson that were priceless.

We worked more problems on his overhead projector than I care to remember and competed them both individually and as a team. We had a point system that was bound by an honor system. We earned up to 5 points for getting the answer the quickest to 1 point for starting the problem in the right way (assumptions, hypothesis, postulates, or theorems). I hated to lose and I admit that I would claim more points at times than I deserved. One point here and one point there added up. I was all about winning but was less than honorable at times. One day Mr. Cates called me on it, for I finished a geometry problem before everyone, even upper classmen. Fortunately, I saw a shortcut that he had never considered before and got to the answer in less than 5 seconds. I did not have the courage to admit that I scalped points but I did stop after he called me out. From that day on, he poured more into me but never stopped trying to convince Mom that sports should not be in my future. I am forever grateful to him and never thought I would be able to tell him that.

Thankfully, I had the privilege of seeing him once again over 20 years later during Easter weekend of 2013. It was an honor to introduce Mr. Cates to Tai and Kennedy. Kennedy finally got to meet the man that inspired and awakened the problem solver in me. However, our meeting was under trying circumstances for us both. Both my dad and Mrs. Cates were in the critical care unit in Baptist Hospital in Montgomery. Dad was losing his battle with cancer, and Mrs. Cates was holding on to life after a car wreck. Under the circumstances, we both were struggling but had a great dialogue about past students, about successes, about failures, and about the future. I was touched again by his conversation, his brilliance, and big heart. The experience took me back to the math tournaments. When we finished the timed tests (no more than 10 problems in 2-3 hours), we would find him (our coach), huddle with him one-on-one, share the experience, and debrief on the problems. Without seeing the problems, he seemed to picture it and walk us through the problem verbally just like any sports coach would. I did not appreciate it then but now know that he was constantly wielding fruit. I took the liberty of sharing what he meant to us as a teacher and how he influenced a generation of students who became lawyers, investment bankers, doctors, Ivy League alum, teachers, entrepreneurs, engineers, and more. I shared with him that his students were grateful for him. No matter their career, most of his students consider him to be the teacher who established the foundation most responsible for their success. Although he would not claim the title, Mr. Cates was transformative for a generation of students that sat in his classroom in a small town.

Mr. Cates encouraged us to ask questions, but my long-time

Chapter 7: Transformative Leadership

mentor, Dr. Gerald Turner, taught me to ask the right questions. Former GE executive, mentee to Peter Drucker, management consultant, executive MBA professor, and brother in Christ, Dr. Turner is amazing. We were introduced by a mutual friend. Leader in the mirror, God places people in your life for a reason. There have been many reasons I can list for Gerald's (he prefers to be called Gerald) place in my life over the years, but in sum, the Lord used him to elevate my game. Although I do not hold an MBA, Gerald has schooled me into one over the years. In every conversation, he left me better than when he found me. He has a knack for asking the most disrobing questions, and that began from the very first time we met. Around 2001, I had developed a business plan to pursue some opportunities in the newly deregulated power market in Texas. The plan had a great story on what was happening with colorful pie charts and waterfall charts to show breakeven. I was so proud of my work and so confident in my spirit. As we sat at the table in the lobby of a Dallas hotel, Gerald took my business plan and my executive summary and placed it to the side. What nerve of him not to look at this awesome work product! Then he asked: "So what?"

I said, "Excuse me?"

Gerald asked again, "So what?"

Dazed and confused, I was speechless. He pierced through my pride, ego, confidence, focus, and faith in the plan with that one disrobing question. He sensed my fluster and asked, "Why this? Why now? Why is it different? Why you? Why me?" Not knowing that he had summed up the "5 Why" principle in one disrobing question: "So what," I managed to follow what he was asking. He wanted me to articulate to him my executive summary of the following:

- Why this?
    - What are you selling?
    - What are you really selling?
    - What is your vision?
    - How will you get there?
- Why now?
    - Who cares?
    - Who has a compelling reason to buy this?
    - What's your go-to-market strategy?
    - What does success look like?

- Why is this different?
  - What differentiates your product/service from other players?
  - What's your "secret sauce" or "special recipe?"
  - Is this advantage sustainable?
- Why you?
  - What is your background?
  - How does it fit your business?
  - What is your story?
- Why me?
  - What are you asking for?
  - If I invest, how much and how do I get it back?
  - What is it in for me?

I learned more in that one session that I had in the last year or so while consuming books on business and becoming an expert on business plan software. However, I am most grateful for Gerald not asking the last question, "What is in it for me?" Our relationship hinges on loving God, serving others, and asking the right questions. We start with "What if" and end with a prayer. Even during his toughest times over years, he never said "No" if I needed a moment to bounce an idea or to talk. I am not sure how to best articulate what Dr. Turner has meant to me. During his career and life, Gerald has sought to serve God first and to serve others before serving himself. He does not seek glory for himself. He is a coach, a mentor, a friend, and a mirror holder. He helped me look at the leader in the mirror. He believes in servant leadership and walks it out every day. When I went to him about CUE Leadership, I was ready for his questions. They had become a part of my DNA.

However, the test came in my first workshop (which I now call Huddles) to introduce CUE Leadership. I had about 12 leaders whom I knew in attendance, and all were older than me. Gerald was front and center and the first to arrive. He was my benchmark, considering that he lived this work and that he taught about corporate transformation every day. How could I tell my mentor was leadership was? How could I disrobe *him* with *my* content? What would he question? It went amazingly well. I followed the formula of establishing **Common Ground** on enhancing leadership, I **Unified the Thought** we needed to close gaps in our own leadership, and I **Equally Yoked** them to the concept that the Word provides the answers in Nehemiah. After that, Gerald immersed himself into first learning more and second to finding gaps. He made great insights, but he made one observation that I was not ready for. He said that pastors, especially those in megachurches, would not embrace this work with open arms. It was his view that pastors would view helping church goers find their purpose as a threat, i.e., lead them out of the four walls of their church, move from under their influence, and most of all, decrease the offering plates. Sadly, he was right. My experience has been just that.

This all led to Gerald's toughest questions... why should people, pastors, and leaders care? Why now? I was partially ready, but here is what I should have articulated.

For:
- ...People from all walks of life—How to build foundational trust and foundational discipleship; including how to protect your blind side or understand if you are a chaser or a magnet.
- ...Pastors and church leadership—How to shift focus from church business to the business of the church; including how to create disciples instead of pew hosts and to help new believers grow.
- ...Any leader—How to understand his or her gifts, purpose, and calling.
- ...Corporate and business leaders preparing for change—How does the Me-Now culture impact culture; including how to build teams.
- ...Other institutions—How to strengthen leadership, decision-making, and accountability among players, employees, or children.

When Gerald asked in so many words, "Why you?" I said that I did not know but was humbled that God chose me for this task. I did not always exhibit humility, although I claimed to be humble. Perfecting it is the goal, but progressing toward it is my journey. First, I had to confront the reality that I was not in control. I took Philippians 4:13 to heart: "I can do all things through Christ who strengthens me," but I claimed the glory instead of giving God the glory. My sister Gladys, our family's first spiritual warrior, spoke these words into me like I was the nail and she was the hammer: "You didn't do it. God did." My flawed logic was that He strengthened me and did these things through me. But she did not give up. She pounded those words into me because she saw something that no one else saw. She called me the "little preacher" at an early age, when I would go to church by myself. I would walk the mile or so on Sunday mornings alone, even if no one else was going.

God can use anyone and anything to move us, even a southern belle. Gladys' nickname is Scarlett, for she was our southern belle. She was just like Scarlett O'Hara in *Gone with the Wind*, for she had talent for marketing, business, and leadership. Gladys was always, always... always in the mirror. No matter what she was doing, she had to find a mirror. Gladys was an Army Captain and spent countless of days in the field. How did she survive in the Army fields without a mirror? She worked hard at chores just like the rest of the family on the Poole plantation. (Ask me sometime about the fried hen dinner.) I guess if Scarlett O'Hara could do it, our Scarlett could do it.

Gladys has the remarkable ability to understand the motivations and feelings of herself or others. She has discernment, thought of others, and shows honor and kindness. She has zeal, drive, and passion that is infectious. I saw it firsthand whether I wanted to or not, but particularly during the summer before I entered high school. She had dreamed in her mind that I needed endurance to match my speed. I told her that I did not need it, mainly because I knew where it would lead. Maybe, I should have used the "Frankly, my dear..." line. Gladys forced me to join her for her daily PT (physical training) when she was home on leave that summer. PT was brutal for the first week and a half. I stopped quite a few times those first couple of days. By the end of the week, she would look back, find me walking, and double-back to urge me. "Come on, you can do it!" she pressed as she ran behind me. She acted like a drill sergeant forcing me to keep up with her. I tried explaining to *Lieutenant Powell* that I was not legally under her command. That did not work. Something changed by the end of the next week. My body was beginning to get a second wind after the first mile and by the third week, I was keeping up with her. On the last days of her leave, I even had a kick at the end. Amazing! Gladys was right. I needed that type of workout.

When Gladys got passionate about something—career, decision, training, or whatever—there was nothing that could change her mind. After journeying through a traumatic experience, she promised her

Chapter 7: Transformative Leadership

passion, zeal, service, teaching, persistence, and her voice to God. Since that day, Scarlett professes that there are no other choices than the ones God wants her to make. In that, she stands steady in any wind, for she is anchored in the Lord. He took the tears that flowed from her after watching Christ being crucified on the made-for-TV movie *Jesus of Nazareth* and turned them into powerful rain that would bear fruit and share the Gospel.

If you don't understand, just ask her to pray... I did. I asked her to offer the opening prayer at Pops' funeral in April 2013. She said that she would not be able to do it, but I encouraged her, I told her that she would have the strength. I said, "You can do it," and she reluctantly agreed. It was time, and she was called up to pray. Before she stood up, she began to sing, "Our God is awesome. He can move mountains, keep me in the valley, hide me from the rain; Our God is awesome, heals me when I'm broken. Strength where I've been weakened, forever he will reign. Our God is awesome. He can move mountains, keep me in the valley, hide me from the rain; Our God is awesome, heals me when I'm broken, strength where I've been weakened, forever he will reign. Our God is Awesome, Awesome, Awesome."

As the church joined her in the Charles Jenkins song, there was power in that place, there was healing in that place, there was strength in that place. She reached down deep to bellow out those words. She reached some fierce pains, not only because Dad had lost his battle with cancer but from her own secret. Two days prior, she had been diagnosed with breast cancer. She was already broken and now had an additional mountain growing inside of her. None of us knew, but the depth of her prayer came from strength not sorrow or weakness. The power in her prayers was truly God's anointing on her spirit. I sensed that no one wanted to follow that prayer, not even the pastors. We could have gone to the cemetery to lay Pops to rest after that. Fast forward a year and a half, the Lord healed her, and she is cancer-free today. Gladys has a powerful testimony and will tell you that one word that describes her best is "Overcomer." She has overcome so much through love, surrender, and prayer. Just ask her to pray.

I share a bond with all my siblings, but Gladys and I share a spiritual bond that started a long time ago. Just like she was a catalyst to build my physical endurance, she allowed the Lord to use her as an instrument build my spiritual muscles, endurance, and growth. She taught me how to tap into discernment and how to understand God's anointing. We pray together now as we did before every college game. Our Saturday morning prayer became an event. It morphed from just the two of us, to adding my roommate Jason, then my friend Rodney, then our quarterbacks Chuck and Corky, then other position players, and then most of our dorm floor All would pack in my dorm room waiting by the phone to hear "Lil' E's sister's prayer" before walking to the Fieldhouse to play. It was amazing.

She and her husband opened their Mt. Pleasant, Texas home to me as I started my career at a power plant with a major utility company. Shortly after I'd arrived, she blessed me with a gift, my personal Bible, engraved with my name. She guided me during the toughest times when I had an infant spirit, which is the most vulnerable time in any spiritual transformation. But she pressed, pressed, and pressed, and I thank God for her persistence.

Just like Scarlett O'Hara, she has been the glue for our family through her leadership and commitment to God's word. Gladys has been an instrument in breaking cycles and an example of staying faithful during good and bad times. Frankly, she has been gathering scattered souls in our family for years. From Gladys to a new generation of spiritual warriors; from John the Baptist to Jesus; from Frederick Douglass to all human rights leaders; from Moses to King David; from Barbara Jordan to educational leaders; Stephen Biko to Nelson Mandela; Robert F. Kennedy to nation healers; from Vernon Johns to Dr. Martin Luther King, Jr.; from Ezra to Nehemiah; from Eleanor Roosevelt to Tuskegee Airmen; from Jim Cates to numerous critical thinkers; and from Dr. Gerald Turner to countless pupils; what distinguished these as transformative leaders was that they were seed, sower, and the soil. Seeds are not meant to lay dormant. They mut be awakened by the living water of Christ and are always looking for a place to be planted. As sowers, they walked the straight path while plowing through with faith, planting seeds of goodness, and pouring the living water of Christ into others. As the soil, these transformative leaders accepted other seeds and absorbed the living water which provided the right nutrients at the right time and enabled good works to take root. When the finished product is mature, the new growth can stand firm and bear new fruit.

Chapter 7: Transformative Leadership

Does this describe the leader in the mirror?

Are you engaged in someone's transformation or preparing a place for new leadership? Are you pressing like Erza? Ezra, one of the greatest men in the Old Testament, was high priest, leader, and writer. He was a direct descendant of a priestly family that included Eleazar, Phineas, Zadok, and Aaron (Ezra:7:1-5). Ezra had zeal for God, loved God's Word, and was persistent in studying and teaching (Ezra: 7:10). God recognized Ezra as a man of discernment (Ezra: 7:25, 9:3). God promised the people of Judah He would return them to their ancestral homeland. With the temple destroyed, God used Ezra's zeal to begin the process of gathering his scattered people who were in Babylon. After 70 years in captivity in Babylon, Ezra was sent by God to rebuild the temple and restore proper worship on the first trip. Worship is at the center of any transformation—the catalyst to rebirth, the tool to hoe weeds, and the root to sustain. Although the physical temple was complete and operational, Ezra's purpose was not complete. God found his people in their own Me-Now culture, lacking the proper reverence toward Him, lacking understanding of Him, and lacking wholehearted obedience to Him. God sent Ezra a second time to restore the spirit temple of His people by admonishing and removing sin. Since God works in an orderly way, Ezra's purpose was fixed; be the soil for spiritual growth—family. Family is the field of harvest by which the Lord would bear more fruit for His will to be done. The men of Israel had entered unscriptural or illegitimate marriages with pagan and worldly women. God knew that these unscriptural marriages would weaken the people's resolve to honor Him and to represent Him. The spiritual temples of the next generation were at stake. If the family was not the seed, sower, and soil of God's Word, it would foster seeds of idleness.

We could name a number of transformative leaders and debate the merits of their work to justify their relevancy. However, what is different about the transformative leaders that I shared is that they were doctrinal. These leaders were invested in restoration to an intended purpose; in taking a conventional approach to what has worked and fixing what has not; and in operating as traditionalists to a higher set of ideals. On the other side of the leadership matrix, there are transformative leaders who are revolutionist. In contrast to the doctrinal, these transformative leaders are invested in changing to a new state of existence; in promoting a rebellion against the status quo based on a new set of rules; and in operating as a progressive to a higher state of power. Think of the ones I have shared as well as some of your own—coaches, teachers, family members, presidents, senators, pastors, maybe even the leader in the mirror. Now compare those to the transformation you seek or you oppose. Is the ground work for the transformation closing the gaps or is it rebalancing our Societal Ecosystem? Is the change foundational; i.e., rooted in restoration or a change to God's intended purpose? Another way of asking… were the purposes and body of work of John the Baptist and Ezra restorations to something that existed or a revolution to something new?

Regardless of your answer, when you come to realize that God has given you a specific purpose, you can move forward with confidence. Leader in the mirror, remember one thing if nothing else. No one can get what the Lord has in store for you; only you can miss it. It is up to you; not to do it alone but by, through, in, and of Him. If you fall on the other side of what the world or culture thinks, just fully trust the One who called you. Remember attacks against you are the very reason why our Societal Ecosystem is warped and out of balance. You may be called a radical, a "Jesus freak." Be like the first one, John the Baptist. We don't have to fear the title of radical for having faith in a friend who freely paid a ransom, restored and reconciled us, and who is the most exalted excellent eternal example, acting on our behalf to access His kingdom. Can there be any greater joy or fulfillment in this life than to know God's pleasure and reward awaits you in heaven? Undoubtedly, moments after his beheading the ultimate transformative leader, John the Baptist, must have heard his master say, "Well done!" Will the leader in the mirror hear the same?

Chapter 8:
CHIEF SHEPHERD

CUE LEADERSHIP MATRIX©

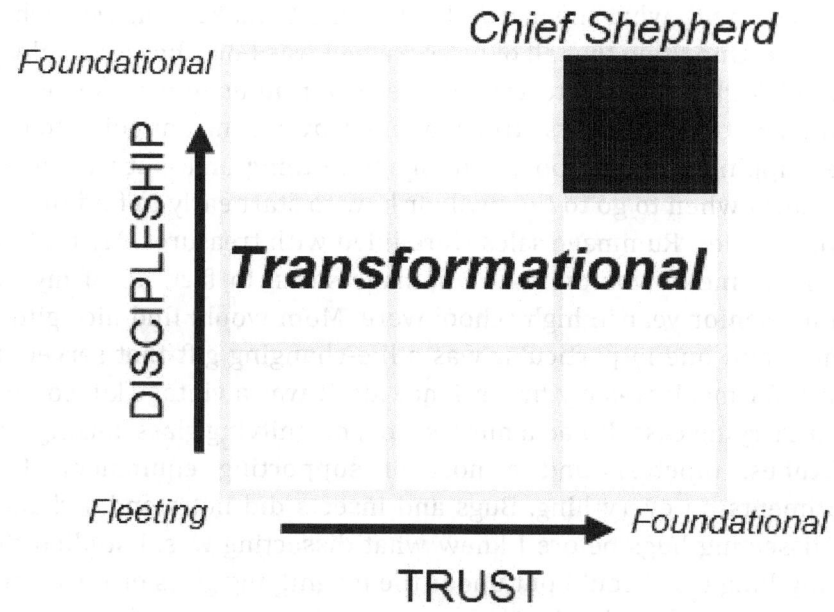

"Can I make my mark?"
—Tom Powell, Jr.

I found it difficult to label our parents or place them in the leadership matrix. Are they Stewards, Transformational, Gatekeepers, or all of the above? I am not sure, but I needed to share some of them with the leader in the mirror...

Mom loves to smile and have a good time. I'm not saying it because she is my Mom, but it is hard to forget her once you've met her. She has an affect on people. I think she could run for mayor of our hometown if she wanted to, for everyone knows her. She is genuine, not

Chapter 8: Chief Shepherd

pretentious. She comes as she is. Mom has a humble, gentle, dove-like soul with an infectious smile that one remembers. Sarah's smile lights up any room, pierces any emotional wall, and delights any wounded spirit. Anyone who knows her will agree. Her smile serve two purposes. When things looked bleak, when we lost a game, when we had no electricity, her smile gave us comfort and encouragement that everything would be OK. Her willingness to sacrifice her own needs, life, dreams, and wants for the good of others is inspiring. Her ability to "make due" with what she had and her ability to make things stretch still amaze me. One thing that all of us cherished was how she could split one stick of Wrigley's gum into enough pieces for all us to have some. Mom could make twenty dollars stretch a long way, if it meant going to every store, clipping every coupon, and buying nothing unless it was on sale. Mom knew when to go to Goodwill or how to start early to find the right rummage sales. Rummage sales were filled with treasures. My first suits were hand-me-downs or from rummage sales. In fact, all of my suits until my senior year in high school were. Mom would find nice gifts for us there and one in particular was a life-changing gift that served as a catalyst for me. It was my first science kit. It was a vintage kit, complete with a carrying case. It had a microscope, magnifying glass, mixing trays, test tubes, pipettes, and a host of supporting equipment. I ran experiments on everything. Bugs and insects did not stand a chance. I was dissecting bugs before I knew what dissecting was. I studied them and anything else I could put under the magnifying glass or microscope. This gift sparked my intellectual curiosity about the world, urged me to ask questions and analyze, and strengthened my ability to solve problems. Math, English, and every other subject were easy for me. That intellectual curiosity was framed and strengthened through my experience at Booz, which then enabled me to dissect the Book of Nehemiah and create our ministry. God is good and purposeful. Mom bought it for $2. She gave the gift to me with a smile, which grew when she saw my face. That was a smile of satisfaction.

That smile has healed many spirits in her lifetime. But as I grew older, I realized that her smile served a second purpose. It was a mask for deep pain. I am not sure where all the pain came from. When we heard her say, "Oh my stars," we knew that she about to either cry or pray. As I got older, I realized that crying and praying was and is the same for her at times. It's her praise. God was her strength to deal with the symptoms and root of her pain. The symptoms were fear, worry, sickness, stress, and even hair loss. I witnessed it manifest itself psychologically (although, not in a bad way). It hurt me, but I finally understood.

We have an entire branch of family that live in Canada. My cousin, Deanna Bowen, who is a filmmaker/history professor in Canada, has tracked over 100 years of her history (our history) from Canada to Oklahoma to Dallas, and back to where our family lived on the plantation in Forest Home, Alabama. She filmed her multi-year journey and shared her documentary at a family reunion in Alabama where our Canadian family joined us in Greenville. It was awesome. After Deanna filmed her first trip to Forest Home, she stopped through Dallas and showed me some footage of Mom and my Aunt Doris. They all visited the "big house," the former Poole plantation home, which was sold some time ago and now operated as a bed and breakfast. My Aunt Doris cooked there, their mother cooked there, and their grandmother cooked there, but Mom had never actually been inside the "big house," only in the kitchen entryway. Like most plantation homes, the kitchen was built as an attachment to the home rather than inside the house. It was connected to the house by a narrow corridor. The rationale was that the kitchen could be easily disconnected to the main home in case of a fire, accidental or intentionally set by a disgruntled cook. Deanna told me that Mom and Aunt Doris did not want to go through the front door and asked if they could enter through the back. Deanna shared that was strange to her until she was filming Mom, and then it all made sense. Deanna showed me the footage of Mom exiting the kitchen and entering the living room in the main house. It brought tears to my eyes as I watched. Mom could not step over the threshold into the living room. It seem as though her leg was chained to something, and every time she lifted her foot, the invisible chain would snatch it back to the floor. Expressions of fear, sadness, terror, and worry were mangled in her face. Tears rolled down her cheeks, and she began to sweat. She started to breathe heavily. She was chained to the past, for she had been forbidden to cross that threshold for years of her life. Nevertheless, I saw her close her eyes and muster the strength to cross that barrier. She broke a chain of fear in the former "big house" that day. If it were possible, I grew even

Chapter 8: Chief Shepherd

more love, admiration, and respect for Mom. She was resilient and persistent. She made due once again. I share this not to embarrass the current generation of the Poole family but to show how Mom overcame her past. Joe Poole, the patriarch, was a powerful man in his time. He was powerful enough to be serious contender for Governor of Alabama in the 1940s. Although Granddaddy Hugh said that he could be a harsh man, our family has a strong bond and love for the Poole family. Being the youngest of 9 children, I knew only a few of them, but have had heartfelt encounters from family members over the years.

"Making due" was no different than what generations of my family had done before. Both sides of my family were still sharecropping in the early 1970s. I am not a generation off the plantation where my ancestors worked as slaves and as freedmen. Both were in servitude and were in bondage of at least the mind and spirit. I struggled for most of my life with that legacy. I was ashamed already with being part of a people kept in bondage for generations. The shame was compounded by the fact that our family did not have our exodus until the 1970s and that our parents were betrothed to that legacy. The betrothal forced us to be a generation behind—economically, socially, politically, and definitely educationally. Mom finished high school, and Dad made it to the 6th grade. Both missed a lot of school due to the harvesting of cotton and missed a lot of life, especially after starting a family of their own. I kid around that Mom was betrothed to Pops since both of their parents played prominent roles in operating the Poole plantation. Just like their parents, they were continuing the legacy of having a big family but not the entire legacy. The legacy included having a big family to work the fields, having enough hands to at least break even on ROIL (return on invested labor), and having enough potential, "sweat equity," to maintain or increase their allocation of land to work. Dad and Mom wanted their kids in school and did not force us to work as they had.

Our parents made it work in the good and the bad times. Mom's ability to make due was always vital, especially when the weather was bad. When it rained, we had little money coming into the house. Pops worked as a logger in the forestry industry after he left the plantation as farmhand. Before he became the best skidder driver in the world, Pops started as a pulpwooder. In logging, the better trees are harvested for sawlogs for lumber production. What's left are the inferior trees and components that are harvested as pulpwood to produce paper products. Most people were happy when it rained, but we knew that Mom and Dad would struggle to make ends meet that week. Dad could not work because of the muddy roads and soggy conditions that the rain brought. Just like the rest of the crew, Pops' pay was based on the number of loads of wood that they harvested. If it rained, no loads could be harvested. If no loads were harvested, Pops received no income. He could not apply for unemployment no matter how long the rain lasted because he was not laid off officially. Cashflow became tighter than it already was, and our parents had to "rob Peter to pay Paul." From missing payments on certain bills, borrowing from friends and family, and getting high interest short-term or payday loans, my folks made due. Much to Pops' objection to taking "hand-outs," I remember standing in line for government food at Lomaxx with Mom during the bad economy of early 1980s. The government was rationing out basic essentials like flour, meal, butter, powdered milk, and the infamous "gov'ment" or commodity cheese that we grew to love.

A little history on that: The cheese was bought and stored by the government's Commodity Credit Corporation and in 1982 was distributed directly to the needy each month under the Temporary Emergency Food Assistance Program of the Food and Nutrition Service. Since Dad was working and not laid off, we were only eligible for a package of powdered milk and two blocks of gov'ment cheese. It was packaged as a five pound block and we sliced it for sandwiches, macaroni and cheese, cheese grits, and cheese toast. A melted slice of cheese on bread was a quick breakfast or after school snack. During that time and afterwards, I thank God for the cheese toast Mom made; the government's free lunch program at school, and our deep freezer! That is why we have a deep freezer in our garage and will always have one. Our freezer took up 20% of the kitchen in our approximately 600 square foot home. It was a necessity during regular times but became our essential lifeline when things got tough. It contained the peas, potatoes, corn, and other vegetables we picked and bagged from the summer; the wild blackberries, plums, apples, and peaches; the deer that we hunted and processed; a few rabbits and squirrels; the nice fat gobbler and hens that Dad stalked during turkey season; frozen milk from a 2 for 1 sale; the fish we caught or drained from local ponds; a mess of quail from the

Chapter 8: Chief Shepherd

fall; sausage, bacon, pork chops, ears, feet, and chit'lins (chitterlings) from hogs we raised and slaughtered in the winter (no mountain oysters... they went fresh to from the hog pen to the pan); or the ground beef, steaks, etc. from a young cow that someone accidently crashed into one evening. You may have called some of those things road-kill, but we called it making due—using what you have.

Through all of this, there was one thing that was consistent—sacrificial love. What was also so loving and sacrificial was that Dad and Mom would eat what was left after we had our fill or would not even take portions at all if we did not have enough to go around.

Our making due was no different from what others have gone through, but sometimes that story is tough for others to relate. I was advising a major healthcare provider on the west coast on how to integrate two performance improvement programs; one developed by corporate and one developed by the collective bargaining groups (unions). Imagine the complexity of the two programs and in bringing an outsider to integrate them. I knew that I had to be open and transparent and listen more than talk (two ears and one mouth)—not to appear to be hiding something. To gain trust with some of the union members, I allowed them to learn more about me by asking about my life and semi-foreign worlds of "Texas" and "Alabama." Once they discovered that I grew up hunting and eating wild game, they peppered me with questions, including asking what animals had I eaten. The list included animals like deer (yes), opossum (no), raccoon (yes), rabbit (yes), eel (yes), snake (no), and others. All was fine until I said "yes" to squirrel. "How could you eat a cute, cuddly thing?" asked a team member. When she discovered that I had eaten squirrel and that I would eat squirrel again, the dynamics of our relationship changed. She was appalled that I had eaten "such a nice creature" and did not understand why I would hunt an "innocent animal." She tried to shame me and rationalize that it was not good because she said that "it had no meat." From that moment on, she could no longer look me in the eye and avoided talking to me. Her point of reference for squirrels were the small little creatures in the park or in her neighbor's tree; and that "hunting" was bad and was only done to mount trophies. How wrong was she? I did not bother to explain how the squirrels in the southeastern U.S. were much bigger, how squirrel hunting was a part of life, and how hunting them helped to preserve people by providing food. None of that would not have helped. I simply told her that it was our way of life and for us it was about survival. We did not have much, but I told her that nature was our grocery store and that we were one paycheck away from financial disaster. In all those items of food in that freezer, there was a story of togetherness, fellowship, love, faith, sharing, and nurturing, as well as survival. I could have told her about the time that I was shocked by the hot wire as a 400 lb. mother sow was after me when we separating her from her young (I practiced my quickness and hand-eye coordination when chasing small piglets). I could have told her about the early morning hunting trips to the Miller Ferry dam on the Alabama River. (This hydro-powered dam is what sparked my interest in the power market.) I could have told her about the time Pops almost burned down Tom's shed from a grease fire. ("Now that was a *farre!*") I could have told her that I don't eat chit'lins now because I had to clean them before we made our own sausage. I could have told her how my shotgun pellets ricocheted off the rock and peppered Tom's arms when we were rabbit hunting. (Needless to say, I was sent to fetch the truck.) I could have told her about my first Zebco 33 fishing rod that Pops pieced together to get me in our family fishing competition. (We competed against each other on everything.) Or I could have told her about how Ma Teet (Grandmother Ethel, Pops' mother) cleaned, battered, cooked, and served me my "kill" for lunch one day; a robin that I shot with my Daisy BB gun and had left on the ground to go shoot another. (I learned a tasty lesson on protecting God's creatures... eat what you kill.) I could have told her all those stories and more, but that would have done nothing for me to gain common ground.

We had some tough times but we made it work, regardless of the fact that my parents supported 10-12 of us on $25,000 or less a year. One would think things would get easier as kids left the house, but our dollar stretched shorter and shorter. The added testosterone of teenage adolescent boys made for some potentially volatile situations. Either it was talking under our breath, missing a time to water the hogs, or picking enough peas, many things compounded our financial stress, including health issues. All of which placed significant strains on our parents' marriage.

"Honor thy father and thy mother, so days may be long," Mom

would say with endearing desperation. If I heard it once, I heard it a thousand times. She knew that the quote went in one ear and right out the other at times. But she said it often with the hope it would stick. If it didn't she would hit us with another one, while pointing her finger, and say, "You will have to give account for yourself to God." She reminded us of these things regardless of the current financial struggles, rainy days, and making due with less and less.

When I was in the eighth grade, at one point all three of us sons were on crutches. I had stressed some ligaments in a junior high basketball game. To add to it, the coach left me at the school without taking me to the doctor or notifying my parents (this still bothers Mom today). After being in a cast for a month and in a splint for a month, Mom finally convinced a doctor to agree to perform the orthoscopic surgery. Sadly, we were turned away by two hospitals because our insurance did not cover the surgery. By God's grace, Coach Elston Turner convinced a doctor in Selma to perform the surgery and allow my parents to pay on an installment plan (pay what we could). I am sure it was the smile on Mom's face and in her spirit that negotiated the deal. Nine years later, after a great high school career, two college national championship games, and a bachelor's of science degree, I paid off the remaining balance with my first month's pay from my first job out of college. I remain thankful.

A few weeks prior to my injury, my brother Jody was also on crutches following a motorcycle accident. This accident added fuel to kindling in our house because it could have been avoided. We were almost done with a game of hoops on the Field. As the game was finishing, our cousin, Buster, drove up on Uncle Hugh's motorcycle. Uncle Hugh, Mom's younger brother, only rode on Sundays and forbid Buster from riding, especially when Uncle Hugh was not home. Uncle Hugh was at work at the time.

"Com'on Joe. Ride wit' me," Buster said in his quick, comforting, and convincing tone. Of course Jody agreed, but I immediately asked Jody not to go. Buster could not drive well, had no license, and was defying Uncle Hugh's wishes. Everyone, I mean everyone, on the Field knew this. Jody pushed the basketball into my stomach and jumped on the back of the motorcycle with Buster. I immediately tried to pull him off the bike, and then bucked up to him. "Get off this bike," I said to Jody.

I told them both that they knew what Uncle Hugh had told Buster.

"That's why you cut through the back of his house and through the field to avoid being seen by your grandma."

I growled at Jody, "Dude, don't get on this bike!" I was determined to fight him, knowing that he would not fight back and would have to get off the bike. Jody and I had never fought before, but he knew I was serious. Then he got a reprieve.

"Y'all stop showing out. Y'all know that Miss Sarah and Mista Tom don't want y'all actin' up," Miss Mae Lee Crenshaw said. Miss Mae Lee was right. I hesitated with my onslaught of words and arm-pulling, and Buster took that opportunity to hit the gas and drive off... with my brother.

As I walked home through fields of soy beans, peanuts, corn, watermelon, and sticker briars, I heard the motorcycle scream up and down the highway. Buster and Jody screeched up the hill toward town. The sound grew faint after a time. As I walked with the basketball in hand, I hoped that Mom would not ask me where Jody was. Then, I heard something strange. The motor revved-up as if it was coming back toward home, but the sound stopped. I slowed my walking pace to see if they would return down the hill. They did not, and I got worried. Little did I know during that five-minute walk (which I had stretched out to ten minutes) Mom already found out that some young boys had wrecked. Someone had called Aunt Fox's house and told my cousins. We did not have a telephone at the time. My Aunt Fox sent my cousin JT down to tell Mom. She was already outside waiting with worry, anger, concern, prayerful, and disappointment—all in one look on her face.

Then, JT shot back out of the house again toward our house. I had seen that run before when he really had something to tell. "Aint Sarah, Aint Sarah, Jody and Buster had a wreck. They done wrecked Mista Hugh Mack's motorcycle," shouted JT breathlessly.

My worst fear had come true. My mother continued to pray to our Heavenly Father. She did not ask JT if anyone was dead, for her spirit told her otherwise. After hours in the emergency resetting a bone in Jody's ankle and placing a few bandages on Buster, Jody came home. Then Dad came home from work and was not happy. I am sure that he was happy that Jody was alive, but Dad blew a fuse.

"I done told ya' and told yo' hardheaded ***, ov'r and ov'r not get

Chapter 8: Chief Shepherd

on the bike with Busta!" He said a lot more, and then looked at me. "Where waz you?" I was frozen. Then he asked his coined question, "Boy, you deaf? Didn't you hear me?"

I manage to stutter a couple of "I-I-I" out of my mouth. Then classic Jody piped in that I tried to tell him. He saved me from Pops' fury, from having to lie for him, and from having to rat on him. Pops was upset with Jody not making a good decision, having wrecked, adding a hospital bill, and most of all, worrying "Yo' Momma." Dad did not tolerate us bringing new worries on Mom. He liked peace, as he would say. But he and Mom had some dramatic arguments. Just like any sons would do, we would be ready to defend Mom no matter what. That caused more tension in the house, but Jody and I always prayed that it would never escalate. Rarely it did, and I found myself between Dad and Jody a time or two.

For the first half of my life, Pops was the typical provider who was a pure alpha male. He was the ultimate "buck" from the Poole plantation. A tough farmhand with big hands and simple words, Pops also served as personal chauffeur for Joe Poole as well as the main driver to haul cotton, supplies, and other goods to and from the market. Pops liked simple things—a solid color t-shirt, jeans or slacks (I never saw Dad in shorts), boots or dress shoes, and a hat, even after a fresh haircut. He loved playing dominoes and was a shrewd player. To my frustration, I could never beat him and left the table many days hearing a giggle behind me. He tolerated no disrespect from his sons. We could not joke him, on him, or about him, but the girls could. He was direct and shrewd with his words and did not bluff. If he told us that he was going to do something, we could guarantee that he was going to do it and that was the only warning or notification. He was not highly affectionate and was tough on his boys (but let his girls do anything). Like almost every male in our family, Dad drank a lot; no liquor, just beer, and only one brand... Budweiser. Dad had his own personal slogan: "When you are out of Bud, you are out beer."

We all poured down sorrow, pain, and challenges, but none more than him. Pops may have drank 1 or 2 beers a day during the work week and made up for it on the weekends. He was an alpha-male with heavy burdens who drank much. This did not mix well with two adolescent males; Jody and me. It was a setting for a volatile situation. When Jody and I share stories about arguments, challenges, or disagreements about Pops with our older siblings, they cannot relate, since they remember him braiding their hair and going fishing. They chalk it up that Mom and Dad would work things out and we were just two adolescent boys who didn't know our place.

Mom and Dad went through a period in my adolescence where they were withdrawn from each other. I am not sure what happened and was happening with Mom and Dad; I just wanted some peace and to spend time hunting and fishing. I got the nerve up to tell Dad one Saturday morning that he was spending more time with his buddies than with me and Jody. We talked over a beer. Although I do not think that he appreciated the fact that I confronted him, he admired my boldness. It opened the door for us to talk.

Talk we did, and much more because I found a common ground that day. That is, when I shared a beer with him, Pops opened up. We shared many beers over the years, until I quit drinking in 2010. I quit because the Lord showed me that He couldn't take me where He wanted to while I was drinking. Once I quit, I was worried about how Dad would take it, considering that is how we connected for so long. One Friday evening, Mom, Dad, Jody, and I sat outside. Tom arrived and pulled a cooler of ice-cold beer off his truck. He walked up, greeted us, and laid the six-pack on the wooden picnic table. Jody grabbed four and rationed three beers to Dad, Tom, and me. I gave the beer back to Jody. He pushed it back and asked what was wrong with me. To everyone's surprise, I said, "I don't drink anymore."

Jody exclaimed, "Whaaaat?"

And Mom asked, "You done ask the Lord to take it from your lips."

I answered, "Yes Ma'am."

Immediately, she went to praising God for delivering her "baby." She was praising and crying, but in a happy way. I told her that I was only a couple of months in, but I still struggled. As quickly as I finished with my statement, Pops said the unimaginable: "We gon' help you wit' it then. Git dat damn beer out from in front of him!"

Wow! Pops was full of surprises. I thought he would judge me. But our relationship was not based on a cold beer after all. He was proud of me regardless. I like to think that I had contributed to him quitting "cold turkey" a year later, after 60 plus years of downing plenty of beer. His oncology doctor recommended that he change his diet as he began to fight cancer. Pops demonstrated discipline and self-control in doing exactly what his doctor recommended and gave us almost two and a half years after being diagnosed with stage four cancer. After two rounds of chemo and radiation, Pops never lost a strand of hair, was never nauseous, and was never sick until his last days of his life.

He died in 2013. I miss him, but we left nothing unsaid or undone. I spent half of my life *not* trying to be like him, but my life became much easier when I realized that I was just like him. I spent part of that time trying not to be like him ashamed. I was ashamed that he did not have the same education, same job, same resources, same house, or the same manner of speech that my friends' parents had. I was so ashamed that when our fifth grade teacher asked us what our parents did for a living, I remember thinking that I could not tell the class that my daddy was straight off the plantation with a sixth grade education and that he was a pulpwooder! I thought they would laugh and think less of me.

I heard my classmates say their parents had occupations like teachers, doctors, lawyer, longshoreman, foremen, business owners, and more. Then it was my turn, and I had to think quickly. I had it! Tom just entered his freshman year at Auburn University. My research had shown that Auburn had one of the top forestry programs in the country, and my daddy was in forestry. So I had the story... I said something to the effect, "My daddy works in forestry. He went to Auburn and got his bachelor's in forestry." It was the biggest lie said in the Butler County School System on that day. Some of my classmates eyes widened as they heard this lie from the pulpwooder's son. My teacher eyes widened too because she had taught my sisters and brothers. She could have embarrassed me right then, but instead she pulled me aside later to encourage me not to be ashamed of where I came from or of my family.

That talk helped, but a year or so later my shame was challenged again. Dad, Jody, and I went to Auburn to watch Tom play football one Saturday morning. We always arrived early in order to get the tickets and to get out front before the Tiger Walk, where the team would walk from Sewell Hall to Jordan-Hare stadium. The Tiger Walk was something wonderful to experience. We arrived, and Dad I walked to the Will Call window to sign for the tickets. Jody was hanging back, for he was into girls at that point. I hung back purposely for a different reason. Dad told me to keep up, but I still slowed. I knew Dad had to sign for the tickets, and it took a long time for him to do it. So, when he was in public, he would make his mark.

Pops looked back and called me forward to sign for him, but the young lady at the table with the tickets said that an adult had to sign. Dad asked, "Can I make my mark, then?"

She said, "Yes sir! You can."

Pops drew one line and then drew the other crossing line, making his "X"—his mark. Under 12 years old, I was embarrassed and could not look the people at the table or in the line in the eye as we walked away. Pops knew that I was embarrassed. He stopped walking and asked me outright if I was ashamed of him. My heart sank, but he did not let me answer. He said, "I ain't 'shamed of my mark. I am not 'shamed of what I am and can giv' a darn what dem folks think about me." He went on to tell me that he left school to help take care of the family at a young age, not much younger that I was at the time.

"I done lived my life," he said. "Now it's time for you to make your mark. We were all on the farm almost 12 years ago and now we here watchin' your brother, who could not walk without braces, play on nat'l T.V. You can do da same. I ain't 'shamed because I have da smartest and fastest boy here in you. Yes, this my mark. What is yo'rs?"

Pops was shrewd in his challenge to me, as always. I was then ashamed for being ashamed. Pops pierced me with his words and eyes. His eyes were resolute and firm. His last words that morning pierced me deeper as he said, "Last thang: Boy, ya hear me good. You can't go thru life 'shamed of where ya came from!" That lesson haunted me for a long time. He was clear and right, but shame is difficult to overcome.

Auburn games were important, for it was free education for Tom, a chance to break away from challenges, a place to open our horizon to new experiences, and a way out of making due. As I shared earlier, Tom is one of Auburn's all-time greats. He came in as a running back, but someone named Vincent "Bo" Jackson came in as well. Getting moved to defense was where Tom needed to be. He could have left his junior year but chose to stay. In his senior year, he was pre-season All-American but got hurt in late in his senior season playing against Georgia Tech. Touted as the next Ronnie Lott, Tom tore five different ligaments on a fluke play. He actually collided with teammate Alvin Briggs going after

Chapter 8: Chief Shepherd

the same interception. Alvin suffered a concussion, but Tom suffered what proved to be the end of his career. Even though Tampa Bay picked him up two years later, his knees were not strong enough to stay.

Our family had lost our best chance to emerge from financial struggles. But his broken knee was strong enough for at least two purposes:

1. We witnessed, tagged along, joined, and learned from his work ethic. Tom put the work in trying to get back—rehab, pool, weights, running, diet, and focus. Jody and I were not the only ones that shadowed him. Our friends and teammates followed as well. They wanted to know when we would make it to the weight room because everyone wanted to do everything Tom did. He taught us how to put the work in and it spread virally throughout our team and teams to come.

2. I was angry for a long time for taking this opportunity for us to see better days financially. "Why Lord did you rob Tom... and us?" That was my question. God is amazing. He answered it about six years later. I was home from college, and we all had a cook-out. I was on the grill with Tom. I witnessed something that I thought I would never see. My nieces and nephews, led by Marlon, Terrance, and Roderick, were joking Pops about his rough hands, rough feet, and light legs (Dad always wore pants). They were pulling, tugging, and wresting with him. They were hugging on him, and he was hugging back. He was grandfather and father all over again. They prepared fishing gear for the morning, for it was a first fishing trip for some. (Dad reserved the right to take his grandchildren on their first fishing trip.) All that I yearned for as an adolescent, my nieces and nephews were receiving. How was I to feel? Yes, I was a little envious, but that feeling did not last long because God had answered my angry question—*Why Lord did you rob Tom... us?*

The Lord showed me that the financial stability and certainty that the NFL may have provided may have enabled for Mom and Dad to split up when times were tough between them and both seemed tired of the journey. If that would have been, our family would not have been together in that moment. This was my answered prayer. He showed us merciful impact rather than raving increase. Tom's broken knee saved our family!

Dad's 19 grandchildren and 10 great grandchildren were his pride and joy all the way to his dying day, Easter weekend of 2013. This was one of the toughest times I had to go through. Tai, our kids, and I were due to travel Thursday morning to Alabama for Easter to check on Mom who was recovering from pneumonia. I was connecting in Charlotte and realized that I would get home too late Wednesday night to catch an early flight Thursday morning to Montgomery. I called the airlines to move the flight to Thursday afternoon. On Thursday afternoon, we went to the DFW airport. Much to our surprise when we arrived, we had no seats on the Thursday afternoon flight! The agent told us that the flight was booked solid. I calmly said, "You are mistaken. You need to check again."

The agent shared that I was on the flight but for the next day. I told the agent that I called to change the time of my flight not the day. She attempted to inform me that it was my responsibility to check the changes. I stopped her mid-sentence and demanded that either she check again or go get her supervisor because I was flying that day.

She said, "I am sorry sir. There are no seats. I am looking right now."

I tried to stay calm and said under my breath, "Lord, get me home." A few seconds passed, I ask her to check again. She did and said, "Wow, where did those come from? Three seats. Let me grab those right now."

"Wow" was the right word. I thanked God! We put Karson in our lap and flew to Montgomery. We arrived in Greenville that evening. Karson was in rare form, and Pops laughed the whole time. He joked with Tai and me that we "could not do anything with her." Karson is a fireplug! About 9:30, Dad said that he was going to bed and that he had laughed enough to last him a lifetime. A little less than 24 hours later, sadly he lost his battle with cancer and was gone! The Lord spared me a lifetime of grief by getting us on that plane. My sister Shari said that he was probably waiting for us, for he had seen and touched all of his children, grandchildren, and great grandchildren (except for one) in the last month or so. I try not to think about it, but sharing his last breakfast with him and his last moments with him may have been unbearable. When Pops went into cardiac arrest, the Lord used that moment to shake my spirit lose. He gave me some fire and renewed vigor to share this Word…

No one is exempt from pain and suffering. There will be seasons of

Chapter 8: Chief Shepherd

life and the timeframe is different for each of us. With all our experience, Tai and I have gone through rounds of "robbing Peter to pay Paul" and "making due." Tai and I have been through more than we would like to admit. I remember Sarah's smile and Tom's mark during these times of uncertainty and fear. They could have become I.D.L.E., and we could have become scattered to the wind. They abided by the school of thought, "do as I say not as I do" because they grew up in the generation that raised children in the spirit of fear and respect. The reason was that if they did not show fear or respect in the South, they may not survive the day... they may not return home alive. Their generation had to stay in their place in order to survive. But as the Word tells us in 2 Timothy 1:7-10, God did gave us a "spirit not of fear but of power and love and self-control."

Pops and Mom managed to do this in spite of their own upbringing in the 1940s and 1950s. They balanced each other. Mom had the humble and loving approach, and Pops had the bold and powerful approach. Pops' tough persona was not fake. I can hear him say, "I ain' scared of nothing but the Lawd. You my boy! You betta not be scared of nothin' either." Through that tough skin, Pops still knelt down and said his prayers every night... He make a mark!

He made his mark on many, and it was apparent at his home-going services that we (the sons and daughters) were not the only ones who felt that way. Of course, he was good father to us, but we found that he was "father" to many more than just us—nieces, nephews, co-workers, his friends, our friends, and many more. We heard so many stories. From those stories in the days after his passing, we heard that Pops was "coach" on the baseball diamond, on the job, on the fishing pond, in the woods hunting... everywhere he went. But he coached with more actions and few words. We heard that he was a protector; where secrets, life, confidences, weaknesses, and hopes were safe in his hands. He was a counselor, reality-checker, jokester, and even a servant. To our surprise, a stranger he met at the gas station showed up at my parents' home when he heard of my dad's passing. Apparently, Dad had pumped gas for the stranger when Dad saw that the stranger was struggling to get out of the car while on crutches.

As we started to plan for his homegoing service, we almost made a mistake by making it private and not letting others in. We are thankful to God that he showed us early that Pops' legacy of time, words, presence, love, and sacrifice impacted more than us. Besides being our father, Pops was father to a village of people. He owned a stake in many, and they owned a stake in his life as well. Pops is no longer suffering but leaves a long legacy. In all the stories, there was an undeniable sincerity in every word that comforted us and undeniable affection for Pops, especially when they referenced or hailed him by many names—Tommie Lee, Spud, Mr. Tome, Mr. Tom, Mr. Tommie, Mr. Powell, Granddaddy, Daddy, Big Brother, Unk, Uncle Bay. As I shared at his home-going celebration, my Uncle Hugh had it right... he called him "Chief." Can you imagine that? A sharecropper, a chauffeur, pig farmer, and pulpwooder with a sixth grade education was a Chief! He was a leader of our village and CUE'd us up by finding Common Ground with all he encountered; sharing a Unified Thought of leaving people better than he found them; and Equally Yoking us in sacrifice and accountability.

Mom had much to do with his transformation from a shrewd Buck to a shrewd Chief through faith, prayers, and persistence. Her gentle and smiling spirit wrapped with the Word pierced his soul as well as ours. They filled each others' gaps. Their lives are a testimony to what God will do for us that spanned a marriage of fifty-four years. It was not perfect, but was a process to leaving us better. They put themselves before us, sacrificed all of themselves for our wellness. They made sure of our well-being and that we cared about our fellow man. They made sure that we understood the Lord was our well-spring, our source for everything. They made sure that we knew that value of being well-coached—to sharpen our iron by sharpening someone else's iron. Food was not only for the body, but they made sure that we knew that importance of being well-nourished in our souls. They made sure we understood the power of words of encouragement and victory. In times of need, they made us understand that we should keep each other well-protected and well-covered in the present and future. Although Mom and Pops were optimistic about the future, Mom would always preface talk of the future with "if I live Lawd's spare." She reinforced the need to be cautious of talking or boasting of the future, for in her words, "tomorrow was not promised." They were not fearful of the future, but there was no question that our future was their purpose.

Just like Nehemiah, Tom and Sarah were Chief Shepherds who

possessed those six distinctive qualities and who guided us through a variety of challenges. They were true servant leaders and were guided by serving us and sacrificing for us, rather than their own needs. They had uncommon discernment that was rooted in the Lord and made decisions without having the benefits of experience or facts. Time and time again, our parents were as persistent as our toughest foes and challenges. Their persistence was a crucial lesson for us in how to handle issues. Given that my parents bore many cups, they were trustworthy in their service to others, and took their word to others seriously. No one has unquestionable integrity, but Mom and Dad understood the value in redemption and of God-molded integrity. Not constrained by their own philosophies, they united us in love and service for God's purpose, not our own. They held God as the only point of reverence or first filter in making decisions. Although Pops has left us, his testimony of redemption and love of Christ lives with us today. It lives with me, for his last squeeze of my hand before he passed confirmed again his belief. We trusted them, followed them, and never questioned their ability to make due, regardless of the amount of doubt and despair or the amount of shame that we mustered. Does the leader in the mirror garner that type of foundational trust and foundational discipleship? Does the leader in the mirror have those six distinctive qualities? If the leader in the mirror has these anointed qualities, can she transform the lives of her children with a smile or can he make a mark on his sphere of influence?

Chapter 9: TRANSFORMING THE LEADER IN THE MIRROR

"Who was this guy?"
—Tai Pentecoste Powell

There were seasons when I looked in the mirror, I only saw the acne-filled, the baby-toothed smile, and the Tommie-Lee head. I saw a reflection of someone trying to be someone he was not, trying to fit in everyone's circle, trying to be liked by everyone, and trying not to be himself.

There were seasons when I became whatever suited me in the moment. From the choir boy, the militant, peacemaker, boy scout, wanna be thug, to the player, winner, Little Giant, or "buck," I was a chameleon. I was always "in Rome." In a post-game interview in college, I told a reporter, "I am whatever the coaches say I am." Yes, I was a team player, sacrificed for the good of the team; I ran from the stardom but wanted stardom. Having no anchor, no identifty, no purpose, and no favor, I chose a variety of cups except the one that was appointed to me. Running from that appointment and chasing something that was not of God, I was always trying to prove something and show that I was different from what I really was.

I was confused and wandered for a long time, all the while thinking I was something. The Word of God shares in Galatians 6:3: "For if anyone thinks he is something, when he is nothing, he deceives himself." That was me. I had many faces in many seasons on the border of dysfunction, masking my anger, shortcomings, shame, deception, and fear—all toxins that me tossed from experience to experience. I was running, chasing, and yet following. I got to a dark place when I was in college, especially after my concussion. Failing and desperate, my world became about me. Whatever I was chasing became my god... what I revered for that season.

My ever-changing point of reverence and confused identity

matched with an unclear purpose infused a sense of unblessedness. I was in mental, physical, and spiritual bondage. I prided myself in being able to look in the mirror first to do a self-assessment before blaming others or making excuses. Proverbs 27:19 shares, "As in water face reflects face, So the heart of man reflects man." I could see that my heart was hard, but I did not have the right lens in order to *really* see. Thankfully, God did not give up on me. About the time after my last college football game and Mom's speech when I was in the "wilderness," the Lord sent me some new lenses. Not the prescription DeWayne Wayne glasses I sported but the lens of an angel—Tai Pentecoste.

    I did not deserve her, but He sent her. She was cute, sassy, smart, tenacious, loving… I tried to find every excuse not to like her. I only found fault in her baggy jeans, hat pulled, Timberland boots, looking like the R&B singer Aaliyah. Coming from Chicago to Jacksonville, Alabama, was a long way for a young woman, especially after just losing her father and brother in a 3-month span. When I first met her, I thought she was just a stuck-up pretty face that did not realize that "bougie" did not work in Alabama. Now that I know what I know, Tai was having one of her migraines on the day I met her. I forgave her for being seemingly snobbish. Throughout my own dysfunction, she returned the favor of forgiveness a few times over the years.

    We hung a lot. I liked her but thought I had too much baggage to truly allow her in. One Saturday afternoon, we sat in my dorm room eating one of Dominoes' $5 large pizzas. (I spent my last $5 dollars, which was supposed to last for another week and a half.) Tai took my high school year book off the shelf and began to flip through it. I puffed out my chest just a little, for I knew that she could not turn too many pages that did not have me on it—Class President, Honor Society, Beta Club, Math Team, Mu Alpha Theta, Spanish Honor Society, S.A.F.E., Prep Bowl, Best Personality, Football, Track, Baseball, Drama, Fellowship of Christian Athletes, on and on… I was the man! (So I thought.) She flipped through and would ask questions about certain pictures and moments. Then, she came to a page and asked, "Who is this guy? He looks familiar. I know him from somewhere." I told her that she couldn't possibly know anyone in there. She replied, "No, I am serious. I think I know him. Come. Tell me who he is."

    I said that I was not coming over there because she could not possibly know anyone from Greenville, Alabama.

"Will you just come and see?" she asked firmly. I begrudgingly stood up and walked over to see this mystery person that she thought she knew. I walked over and was surprised at the place where her finger was touching. Tai had her finger on our cap-and-gown picture, but more specifically on my image on the front row. I had almost all the honors that one could get. Then she asked two piercing questions: "Who was this guy? What was he thinking at that moment?" The questions were piercing because I had not lived up to the expectations set by that leader in the book. The leader in the book had plans to conquer the world and be great. That leader in the book was anchored, knew who he belonged to, and had purpose. That leader in the book was the "best of us." The leader in her lens was not that leader under her finger. Talk about confronting a reality! Like the prodigal son, I was waddling in mud and eating from a trough of *less*ness. And Wow! Tai was more than just a pretty face. She had potential. She was a messenger. She was a gamechanger for me. She did not call "fair catch" and accept where I was in life, she did not allow me to call "Peter" anymore, but decided to get me back to the wall. The Lord used her to slay and tame the lion that was somewhat out of control.

Tenacious and an expert debater, she has forced me to confront the reality of my own self-imposed weights—making me laugh, not taking myself so seriously, and feelings of being undeserving of good things. I will place her in a debate against anyone... anyone. But she missed her calling though—comedy. She should be on someone's stage.

What people tend to miss and what I missed at first is her ability to break down walls. I have seen her in action with some of the most snooty, pretentious people. One minute, these people are talking about their private jet and turning their nose up to us wondering how did we get invited to this function. The next minute, Tai has the heiress of a food empire following her and telling her deepest secrets. I don't know how she does it, but I love it and love her.

Tai has seen every season of me—from being poor, depressed, and faithless to those times when I am a leader onCUE for God. She was not with me in my first experience, when the Lord called me before I was ten years old, but she has been there at other critical moments. The first of which was in the spring of 1997. I had moved to Texas but I was

Chapter 9: Transforming the Leader in the Mirror

visiting Alabama for a family and friends church program at my home church, Pine Flat. Tai was still in college but was there with me. During the program my late Aunt Leola, one of Mom's other sisters, was singing my grandpop's favorite song, "He'll Understand And Say Well Done." She had this great soul-stirring voice. She moved the congregation to where a few, including Ms. Oma, were up shouting. They were not the only ones. My Uncle Hugh left with tears in his eyes. He not only left the church but cranked his truck and left. She also stirred something in me. I was overcome with a feeling that I had felt only one time before. I left the church crying and somewhat embarrassed. Tai followed, but I could not face her. Gladys also followed me out. I opened the back of my SUV in order to hide behind it. I could not control my emotions and chalked it up as being overwhelmed with the grief of still missing Granddaddy, but the spiritual warrior Gladys knew differently. She knew exactly what it was. Gladys went to her car, got her bottle of oil, and anointed my head. She rubbed my back and prayed over me and Tai. She asked the Lord to prepare, protect, build, and use me for His calling. In her prayer, she asked God to show me my purpose and for Him to remind me of the "lil preacher" inside of me. Then, she began to speak in tongues. I had not ever heard her do that but her words soothed me, even though I did not understand them. When I finally gathered myself, I told her that I was just sad about Granddaddy. I was overwhelmed by grief. That was it. Gladys did not acknowledge my comments but turned to Tai. She asked Tai to cover me because I would need it. Amazingly, Tai was calm the whole time and told Gladys that she would watch me. I did not ask her why she anointed me, for I was afraid of what she would say. I did not want the cup.

Fast forward to my eldest daughter's *Passion* play about 4 years ago. The Spirit stirred me as I watched a kid carry the cross as Jesus. I was overwhelmed with the presence of the Spirit, told Tai that I would be back, and left the church. I told God that day that I heard His reminder.

I got another true awakening when Dad flat-lined in the hospital. God gave me some fire. I can't explain it, but it took away some inhibitions that I had. I knew God was taking me through a makeover.

Then, I got a cleansing and a refreshing prior to my prayer at my uncle's funeral. I asked for strength to speak and resolve not to allow

Satan to take over me, for I could feel the wounded souls in the church. The secret still lingered, I could feel the pain and anxiety of those He hurt, but I needed to share words of forgiveness, redemption, and life. I told those gathered about my uncle's redemption through his relationship with Christ and how freeing forgiveness is. He caused great pain, but God's grace through Jesus was greater. Tai was not there, but she knew what I was going through.

But the all the inhibitions came crashing down because the Lord took over one morning after a time of personal morning prayer. If I had any doubt if the Lord was real, if I could have a personal relationship with Christ, if the Holy Spirit was real, or if I could have communion with Him, all doubts would have been washed away. The Lord gave me my own Pentecost moment. I could no longer resist or suppress the Spirit of God as I had done the times that I referenced above. The Spirit took over. Not to compare God's Spirit to fleshly pleasures, but that experience was more overwhelming that any other fleshly pleasure that I had ever experienced.

My praise woke Tai, who scrambled franticly through the double doors to our bathroom. God showed me some of His power, but just as important, He showed it to my good thing, my help-mate... my wife. The former Tai Pentecoste and I experienced my Pentecost moment together. He answered my prayers to Him, asking Him to reveal what He was doing with me, to reveal that He was indeed making me over, and to reveal my new birth in Christ. Tai rubbed my back for 15 minutes as the Spirit continued to fill me completely. As He used her almost 20 years prior to look in the mirror and confront and calm vigor of an untamed, angry, and preyful Eric, she experienced Him give that vigor back to a more tamed, hopeful, and prayerful "lion from Zion," not by the flesh but by the Spirit.

The Lord can use instruments from all types to relieve, restore, and refine you. The instrument could be someone like my wife, who helped me confront the realities of the toxins that ran through my spirit. It could be a moment like the many I had reading with my one and a half year old daughter Kennedy to restore an intangible gift—my ability to absorb content almost as well as I could prior to my concussion (from college). Or perhaps the Lord will use someone like my daughter Karson who injects new life, love, fun, and infectious passion into my spirit and

Chapter 9: Transforming the Leader in the Mirror

into our family. She certainly injected those things into Pop on his last day.

I grateful and thankful in God's gift of Tai, our girls, our parents, the leaders (named and unnamed) in this testimony, and you.

And leader in the mirror, if you wonder if Jesus is real... Ask Him to reveal Himself to you through the filling of His Spirit. I know now that He had been trying to give me that experience since that day on the road to Mt. Zion church, but I did not surrender to it. His revelation to me has been progressive. He's taught me more about Himself through the years and as I've allowed myself to be open to His lessons. What I am most thankful for is what our Lord, Jesus Christ grants us every day—a second chance. As long as one can see the leader in the mirror, he/she has a second chance to experience His love and mercy; to do His Will; to have the indescribable feeling to know what your purpose is; to overcome bumps in the road and failures; to heal from brokenness; to experience His joy; and to perfect holiness.

What does second chance mean to the leader in the mirror? Well, let's see what the Word of God says about second chances. In Ecclesiastes 9:11 King Solomon shares: "I have seen something else under the sun: The race is not to the swift or the battle to the strong, nor does food come to the wise or wealth to the brilliant or favor to the learned; but time and chance happen to them all."

We find that Solomon is using his own experience to explain this. I believe he is sharing that success is uncertain and provides more evidence that man does not ultimately control events or circumstances. The race does always go the swift. Battles are not always won by the largest number or the best-trained troops. Gideon's story is a very good example of that. He took 300 men and whipped thousands of the enemy. If God chooses, then His Will will be done. And if by chance the leader in the mirror is in His Will, then all the better.

Second Chance

If you look in the dictionary, you'll find multiple definitions for the word "second" and the word "chance."

First, let's examine "second" as an adjective:
1. Coming after the first in order, place, rank, time, or quality.
2. Inferior to another; subordinate. (Second vice president at the bank; a leader second to none)

As a noun, "second" means:
1. One that is next in order, place, time, or quality after the first.
2. An article of merchandise of inferior quality.
3. In music:
    a. The interval between consecutive tones on the diatonic scale.
    b. A tone separated by this interval from another tone.
    c. A combination of two such tones in notation and harmony.
    d. The second part, intrument, or voice in a harmonized composition.
4. An utterance of endorsement, as to a parliamentary motion.

What does "chance" mean? As a noun, "chance" means:
1. The unknown and unpredicatable element in happenings that seems to have no assignable cause or a force assumed to cause events that cannot be foreseen or controlled; luck. *Chance will determine the outcome.*
2. The liklihood of something happening; possibility or probability. *Chances are that you will win. Is there a chance of rain?*
3. An accidental or unpredictable event.
4. A favorable set of circumstances; an opportunity. *A chance of escape.*
5. A risk or hazard; a gamble. *I took a chance that the ice would hold me.*

As an adjective, "chance" is something caused by or ascribable to something. A chance encounter. A chance result. I've adjoined some of these definitions to give us a purposeful meaning as it relates to how God sees us.

For the leader in the mirror, **second chance** means getting in perfect harmony with the first order of things via an indescrabable force to bring forth a set of favorable circumstances in the right season. In other words, you have the second chance to transform yourself for God's Will—not for you, but for Him, His will and His will alone—to correct this I.D.L.E.ness, to stand apost as a gatekeeper, to commit to your assignment, to be excellent, to perfect holiness, and to lead where you are.

Chapter 9: Transforming the Leader in the Mirror

Leader in the mirror, no matter your failures, mistakes, worries, fears, situation, or circumstances, the Lord can shift your situation if you first get on CUE with His will. However, that order has to be holy, not perverted like the order we have in our Me-Now culture. How to get a "second chance?" How to "get in order with an indescribable force to bring forth a set of favorable circumstances in the right season—not for you but for Him, His will and His will alone?"

There are 5 variables in the formula. They are elusive if not placed in proper order. They are based in the Book of Nehemiah and are confirmed throughout the Word of God.

I like how the wise King Solomon puts it in Ecclesiastes. He teaches that a life not centered on God is purposeless and meaningless. Without Him, nothing else can satisfy the leader in the mirror. With Him, all of life and His other good gifts are to be gratefully received, used, and fully enjoyed. True pleasure comes only when we acknowledge and revere God. This reigned true with Nehemiah. When he heard about the crisis among his people, he did not rush off into frantic activities trying to do something, nor was he idle. Instead, Nehemiah stopped, wept, fasted, and prayed. In his prayer, Nehemiah first offered reverence because he revered the Lord as he began: "God of heaven, the great and awesome God, who keeps his covenant of love" (Ne 1:5-6). How does that translate to getting onCUE… a second chance?

1. Point of Reverence

The first variable in the formula is to have the right **Point of Reverence**. Nehemiah knew that his first step in the decision-making process had to be anchored in the Lord. He also knew that God was the only source that would ensure success and would endure through the good and tough times. As he has done before, Nehemiah set his compass on God in all of his decision-making and knew that his steps had to ordered by God, not by the other gods of the world. Leader in the mirror, where is your compass set? I'm not asking where you *hope* it to be, where is it truly set?

Do you serve the god with little "g" or the Big "G?" Leader in the mirror, consider these IF-THEN statements:

IF your life is all about you; if your decisions are based on your current circumstances or what's in it for me (WIIFM); if you deny yourself a pleasure, pride, or other things for your own righteousness; if you call your friend, wife, spouse, or anyone else first for help in your circumstances; and/or if you depend on "self-help" to endure through tough and easy times, **THEN** your Point of Reverence is on the god of SELF. My life got easier when I realized that my life is not about me. My life is now about doing two things: 1) giving God the glory and 2) serving others. It is that simple. Leader in the mirror, don't worry but rather do as scripture shares in Matthew 6:33, "But seek first His kingdom and His righteousness, and all these things will be added to you." Nehemiah did just that, and the Lord added.

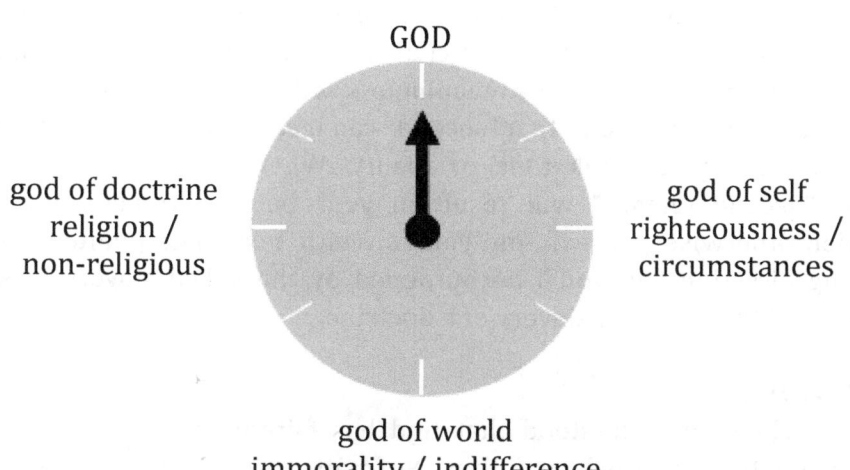

IF all of your passions, time, commitment, and talent are wrapped into worldly things (fast culture, green, career, wealth); if your decision is always based on a world view; if you worry about political correctness; if you search the world's acceptance and admiration in everything you do ("number of likes"); and/or if you have become indifferent to immorality and perverseness, **THEN** your Point of Reverence is on the god of WORLD. Scripture shares, "do not love the world or anything in the world" in 1 John 2:15 and "be not conformed to this world: but be ye transformed by the renewing of your mind, that ye may prove what is that good, and acceptable, and perfect will of God" in Romans 12:2. Leader in the mirror, it is tough to walk within God's will in the world we live in. But do not love the world and do not conform to it, for our generation and future generations are at stake.

Chapter 9: Transforming the Leader in the Mirror

IF your doctrine (religious, politics, atheism) is your complete compass; if your doctrine feeds its own righteousness (increase) or focuses on the differences; if your doctrine closes you off from the world; if your doctrine ignores the greatest of God' commandments... love; and/or if your doctrine forces you to depend on the doctrine, self, world, or a combination, **THEN** your Point of Reverence is on the god of DOCTRINE.

However, **IF** the Lord is all things to you; if the Lord is where your decisions start and end; if the Lord gets the praise and honor and glory; and the Lord is where you draw your strength... no matter the season in good and bad times, **THEN** your Point of Reference is on God with the big "G." In this way, your second chance, no matter how you define it, will not be in vain, will not be meaningless, will not be purposeless.

The dictionary says that "second" can mean "coming next after the first in order, place, rank, time, or quality." When the first order is God, your "Second Chance" will result in your being a transformational leader. Otherwise, you will find yourself with a compass pointed in the wrong direction and you'll be burdened by the yoked slavery of self, slavery of the world, or slavery of a doctrine.

2. Identity

Nehemiah understood that God has faithful love that honors a covenant through thick and thin. No matter the circumstances, God stands on his promises, even though Nehemiah, the exiles, and we do not always keep ours. Therefore, in the second part of his prayer, Nehemiah confessed his sins (Ne 1:6-7). Nehemiah humbled himself as a servant and acknowledged that he was a sinner, not keeping the Lord's commandments. The dictionary defines "second" as "something of inferior quality." I believe Nehemiah understood that he was indeed inferior to God in every way.

Since Nehemiah was anchored in God, he defined his **identity** in God. The Lord made each of us. Accept that or not, we have all been confused about who we are at some point in our lives. We all have people we wanted to be like. We all had a *sense* of who we are, but we all have heard of others saying that "I need to find myself." When we have that mindset, we can go through life chasing everything that looks and feels good; going from situation to situation, chasing broken relationships, or chasing a dream that is not yours to have. Leader in the mirror, the question is not "who you are" but the question is "whose you are?" We all belong to our maker, the Almighty God of Heaven. We were created by Him but CANNOT use the excuse that "God made me this way" regardless of our vices or complexities. God is not the author of this Perverted Order. The Lord is not the author of what Nehemiah confessed about himself; that he was: "a sinner not keeping the Lord's commandments." The never-changing anchor (Mal 3:6), the rock of ages (Ps 138:8)—God is not the origin of this Perverted Order. This began in chapter 3 of the Book of Genesis. God created us in His image. Adam and Eve's disobedience distorted that by introducing sin and perversion into God's creation. How did this happen? It started with deception. The great deceiver Satan, cooked up a cocktail of deceit disguised with some truth from the Word of God. In this blatant denial of a specific divine pronouncement from God, Satan used crafty words of "you will not certainly die," which appealed to Adam and Eve's flesh.

First, temptation is powerful. Temptation can fool us into believing that sinful urges are permissible just because God *made us* or *wired us* that way. Most often, temptation is just like the forbidden fruit. It is good for consumption and tastes good, and seemingly a little bite will not harm anyone. Second, sin is "eye candy" and pleasing to our sight, which is how temptation usually starts. Thirdly, temptation is liberating in that it allows us to gain wisdom and creates new enlightenment. That cannot be all bad. Right? Well, if the liberation, newfound wisdom, or enlightenment takes us away from the eternal anchor, it is purely deception.

Satan's deception perverted the order of a sacred, divine garden that was in communion, fellowship, and harmony with God. Lastly, what does this perverted order birth or create? It creates more of the same and bears the same type of fruit unless the leader in the mirror takes a stand to not conform to this world and is "transformed by the renewing" of his/her mind. To accept how we, the world, or a doctrine defines us does not prove what is that good, acceptable, and perfect will of God.

"Whose you are vs. who you are" is really a question of Spirit versus the Flesh. Leader in the mirror, with whom do you align Truth, Character, Imitation, and Regeneration?

Chapter 9: Transforming the Leader in the Mirror

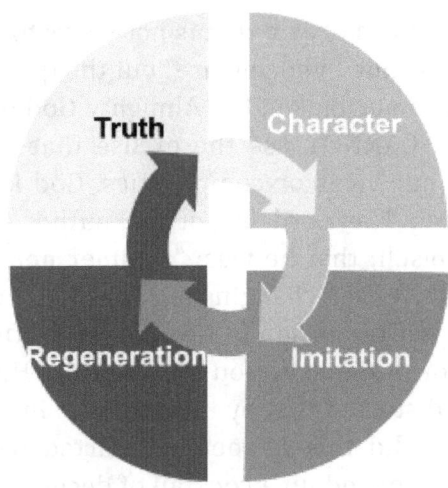

Truth. What you allow to occupy your mind will sooner or later determine your speech and your action. It becomes your truth. Is your truth (speech and actions) noble, right, pure, lovely, and admirable (Philippians 4:8-9) Can you say this about all of your thoughts? Do you have confidence in yourself (flesh) or what that is? Where does righteousness come from... flesh or God? All are questions for the leader in the mirror.

Character. Who or what do you suffer for? Suffering produces perseverance. Perseverance produces character. Character produces hope. Hope does not disappoint us because God has poured his love into our hearts by the Holy Spirit, whom he has given us. A follower of Christ can rejoice in suffering because he/she knows that it is meaningless. It is part of God's purpose is to produce character in His children.

Imitation. How do you know you are in Him? Whoever claims to live in Him must walk as Jesus did. (1 John 2:6) Who are you walking with? What would Christ do? Anyone who claims to be in the light but hates his brother is still in the darkness. (1 John 2:6) Do you do just enough or do more than what is required?

Regeneration. Are you birthing flesh or the spirit in yourself, in your children, or in your sphere of influence? Regeneration is how you improve and sustain a spirit of excellence in your God-given **Identity**. We have to be careful not to change to fit our desires like some leaders change to fit the thought of the day like a chameleon—in stealth mode and disguised in camouflage; changing from color to color depending on the environment; and always in survival mode. Leader in the mirror, be like the butterfly rather than like the chameleon, for regeneration is not about change but about transformation. Change can be turned back or reversed (backsliding). True transformation cannot be reversed if we operate in the Spirit. Once a butterfly is transformed, it cannot go back into its cocoon. We are not made over by our environment, our circumstances, ourselves, or doctrines, but by the Spirit.

In John 3:6-7, Jesus shares with Nicodemus that "flesh gives birth to flesh, but the Spirit give birth to spirit. You should not be surprised at my saying, 'You must be born again.'" The Holy Spirit is sovereign and works as He pleases in the renewal of the heart. Leader in the mirror, ask God to work in you. God needs men and women of valor to stand and to be transformational—spiritual evolution rooted and defined by God and by Him alone.

Leader in the mirror, please get this. Please understand that the creation cannot determine what it was created for. To go through life misusing, "I am who I am," does not keep you in line or in proper order in the formula to get that Second Chance. The Lord will reveal and give you your Identity. Simply, Identity is defined by God, not by self. Leader in the mirror, the question remains… Who are you vs. whose are you?

As Nehemiah continued in his prayer, he asked God to remember the promise of the covenant, asked God to gather a scattered people, and asked God to use him to bring them to a place in His name; not in Nehemiah's name but in God's Name. To "gather a scattered people" was Nehemiah's Purpose. Nehemiah asked God to use him, for he did not want to be I.D.L.E. He wanted to lead a starved, broken, desperate, and isolated people in building a wall around ancient Jerusalem and in essence building "a way of life." He wanted to do something that society said could not be done and that society did not want done. Nehemiah wanted to "bring forth a set of favorable circumstances" for his people, while the rest of society sat idle and I.D.L.E.—standing still in fear, in indifference to what was happening around them, in shame, as well as standing without purpose. This is much like today. Many in the Me-Now culture are standing without purpose.

3. Purpose

Purpose is the next variable in the formula. Leader in the mirror,

Chapter 9: Transforming the Leader in the Mirror

understand that God has a purpose for everyone. Roman 8:28 tells us, "...And we know that God causes all things to work together for good to those who love God, to those who are called according to His purpose." There have been many sermons spoken and many books written on the purpose of life. Pastor Rick Warren wrote a good book years ago (*The Purpose Driven Life*) about leading a life guided by purpose. In short, it talks about finding your purpose and you find it at the intersection of experiences, relationships, passions, interests, education, and resources. There, we are able to solve the mystery of why we are here.

CUE Leadership helps you find purpose a little differently. There is an order to things. Only after having the right of Point of Reverence and understanding your Identity, God can give you your Purpose. Purpose is defined by God, not by you, society, or self. Once you have that order, just as Nehemiah, you can then begin to understand your purpose. Why? Leader in the mirror, Nehemiah knew if he located and began with God, the Lord will reveal it to him. He will provide you resources to help you, and will provide you with a roadmap. An author I had on our onCUE! Radio Show said, "Purpose is caught, not taught."

Although I have been a believer all of my life, I did not know what I did not know. Reflecting on the road that I have traveled, I did not recognize when the Lord moved my spirit and did not have the right "coverage" to help me understand. I did not know how to tap into Christ, did not depend on Him only, and had not began to sync my journey with His will until He began to renew me and rebirth my spirit. The renewal began with "breaking" my dependence on the world and taking my focus off of me. There was a time where I was purely about upward mobility. My dependence and focus were on the next career move, on the next step in getting close to the powerbrokers at my company, on the next increase in pay.

With my career seemingly on the rise at the major utility in 2002, I just had made another career move, frankly because of the pay. The Lord gave me proper warning not to make that decision. Although I did not heed His warning, He gave me answers to the challenges that I was about go through. One day before my career began to fall apart, I was riding on train into work reading Jack Welch's (former powerful CEO of General Electric) book *Straight from the Gut*. I knew all the executives would be reading it too—another one of my moves. A young lady sitting beside me on the train was reading the Bible. She slipped me a note, a gift that I carry with me today. I did not read it then, but read it later in the day, after I got laid off. My mistake was my disobedience and not heeding the Lord's warning. This was the first time in my life where some decided not to like me. I was the only one in the group laid off. The mark of being laid off and not wanted clipped my proverbial wings. Angry, uncovered, shamed... I blamed everyone but myself. That was a tough time for me—spiraling career, molestation memories, financial troubles, marital problems, Pop's stroke, depression... but God gave me a roadmap in that gift on the train. The note was entitled "Hands" and was message from God that I was about to go through some things and that He was the way through.

HANDS

A basketball in my hands is worth about $19.
A basketball in Michael Jordan's hands is worth about $33 million.
It depends whose hands it's in.

A baseball in my hands is worth about $6.
A baseball in Mark McGuire's hands is worth $19 million.
It depends whose hands it's in.

A tennis racket is useless in my hands.
A tennis racket in Pete Sampras' hands is a Wimbledon
  Championship.
It depends whose hands it's in.

A rod in my hands will keep way a wild animal.
A rod in Moses' hands will part the mighty sea.
It depends whose hands it's in.

A slingshot in my hands is a kid's toy.
A slingshot in David's hand is a mighty weapon.
It depends whose hands it's in.

Two fishes and five loaves of bread in my hands is a couple of fish sandwiches.

Chapter 9: Transforming the Leader in the Mirror

Two fishes and five loaves of bread in God's hands will feed thousands.
It depends on whose hands it's in.

Nails in my hands might produce a birdhouse.
Nails in Jesus Christ's hands will produce salvation for the entire world.
It depends on whose hands it's in.

As you can see now, it depends on whose hands it's in. So, put your concerns, your worries, your fears, your hopes, your dreams, your family and your relationships in God's hands. Because it depends whose hands it's in. Have a Blessed Day!

I was to put my concerns, worries, fears, hopes, dreams, family, and relationship in God's hands, because, "it depends whose hands it's in." That gift of encouragement facilitated a gradual rebirth through a period of brokenness—failed business, troubled marriage suppressed memories, financial troubles. He built me back up, filled me with the Holy Spirit, equipped me with an idea, and aligned me with His will... my purpose.

Leader in the mirror, what is your purpose? What would you do every day if money was not issue? Volunteer, paint, or fish? I would coach more leaders in understanding purpose, enhancing leadership, and being one accord with God. What are your three gifts? The Lord will provide you a purpose and He will provide you gifts to confirm it. We have intangible gifts of charisma, speech, singing, etc., but I am referencing the tangible gifts, like those we get at Christmas or what Jesus received at His birth. Christ received three gifts at His birth—gold, frankincense, and myrrh. All three foretold Christ's purpose—gold for He was the one true king, the way, the truth, and the life; frankincense for healing, mending, restoring, and bringing forth new life; and myrrh for anointing His body, for He was to die and pay the price for our sin.

What are your three gifts? That is your task for the coming month. My purpose is to align, equip, and transform new leaders for God's glory.

My three gifts are:
1. Science kit from Mom that had a microscope and magnifying glass

and a host of things to run experiments with.
2. The Study Bible that my sister Gladys bought for me when I first moved to Texas after college. This allowed me to study the Word and make it a part of me.
3. The note from a stranger, giving me answers to my short-term problem of being laid off and to help in my season of brokenness sparked by the memory of being molested.

Leader in the mirror, understand that if you locate God, He will give you the '"roadmap" or gifts, resources, and provisions to support your purpose as he did with Nehemiah. Nehemiah left for Jerusalem with the provisions he needed—letters to ensure a safe journey and to obtain timber for the city gates as well as the protection of a full army cavalry led by officers. These accommodations, authority, and provisions came directly from King Artaxerxes. Having the right Point of Reverence, knowing your Identity, and having Purpose puts the leader in the mirror in proper order.

A renowned pastor that I know put it this way. He shared that "A confused identity matched with unclear purpose leads to a sense of a blessless life." Having things in improper order brings confusion. We can go through life working and chasing significance that is meaningless if we do not go to God first.

One of the definitions of the word "second" relates to music. It reads: "Second is a combination of two such tones in notation or in harmony." Leader, when you have these variables in order, you operate in harmony with the second chance that God grants you.

4. Anointing

What is the "indescribable force to bring forth a set of favorable circumstances?" Nehemiah asked for it when he asked God to let His "ear be attentive" and asked for success in His name. Nehemiah knew that staying near to God would grant divine favor, or the fourth variable in the formula, **Anointing**. It is God's way of covering you, protecting you, and appointing you in His divine way. Some people call it intuition, sixth sense, sacred writ, divine shift, or spiritual quotient. Once the Lord anoints a leader, He will put a hedge around that leader. Absolutely anything is possible at that point with the Lord's will, from parting the

Chapter 9: Transforming the Leader in the Mirror

Red Sea, saving a nation after being sold into slavery, to being chosen as king over all your older brothers. Even before Job went through his trials, Satan had to get permission to go over the hedge and test Job.

But we have to be careful not to self-anoint. We can fool ourselves into thinking that God is finding favor with us and anointing what we are doing. God can only anoint and appoint. If we declare it, we need God's second, His "utterance of endorsement." When we see God's favor or anointing on someone, we usually discover a series of unknown and unpredictable events that seem to have no assignable cause. This indescribable force causes events that cannot be foreseen or controlled. Those who don't follow the Lord may call this "luck." Leader in the mirror, recognize what it is and learn a lesson from King Saul in dealing with the future king, David.

Saul could not accept that the Lord's cup was passing from him. He was envious to the point of trying to stop what the Lord had declared. Leader, you must not envy another's favor but rather be a part the fence that the Lord is building around him or her. David understood this when spared Saul's life, even though David had a chance to take it. The future king said to his men (1 Samuel 24:6), "The Lord forbid that I should do such a thing to my master, the Lord's anointed one, or lift my hand against him; for he is the anointed of the Lord." David knew he was anointed as well, and gave Saul a second chance.

When that indescribable force touches and covers you, it will set forth favor on your circumstances. The anointing is not just for your tangible circumstances but for your entire being, including your leadership. Recall that I began this journey asking a few ladies in St. Louis as to why they were voting for then Senator Obama, which led me to the following questions:

- How do we know when a leader is truly transformational?
- What can we learn from Nehemiah in today's economic, social, educational, and political crisis?
- How did he lead this tremendous change?
- How do today's leaders compare to Nehemiah?
- Can we reconstruct, discover, or identify Nehemiah in everyday leaders to help navigate today's issues?

There are many types of leaders that we have discussed on this journey, but what makes a leader **transformational** is God's anointing.

God's Divine Appointment elevated and illuminated Nehemiah's leadership to transformational status. Nehemiah's ability to garner foundational trust and foundational discipleship from an uncommitted people was nothing short of the Lord working in Nehemiah's favor. The Lord anointed those six key qualities that garnered foundational Trust and Discipleship via...

1. **Integrity** to balance unquestionable versus God-molded integrity
2. **Discernment** to be wise with limited knowledge
3. **Philosophy** to understand if you are a chaser or a magnet for success
4. **Service** to understand if you are powering up or empowering
5. **Persistence** to endure weary feet or a weary promise
6. **Gamesmanship** to protect your blind side

Trust and Discipleship are at the axis of leadership. With these qualities, Nehemiah managed challenges that directly and indirectly affected him, including challenges from the people he led. Nehemiah managed the circulating lies that he was accepting kick-backs in exchange of favors; battled the practice of mortgaging lifetime human labor for meat and other basic essentials; secured the economics (fish and spice trades) as the first step in nation-building before solving social, educational, and educational issues. Nehemiah led the exiles in rebuilding the walls of Jerusalem while navigating them in times of doubt and despair—much like modern-day issues and challenges in America and abroad.

How did he manage to accomplish this as well as to maintain a sense of duty, ownership, and perseverance during the tough and challenges times? God's favor, God's anointing, granted him a presence, an elegance that many seldom experience. He garnered trust and discipleship and ensured that the exiles were onCUE, even in times of doubt and despair. Our Societal Ecosystem is warped out of balance because of irreverence to God (His presence, power, knowledge, dominion, love, and wrath).

Leader in the mirror, He will do the same for you. God's anointing can raise you from dysfunctional to transformational and can lift the

Chapter 9: Transforming the Leader in the Mirror

self-imposed weights that hinder your ability to be effective in the perverted order that exists in our Me-Now culture. These are the qualities that allow you to build the Common Ground, Unified Thought, and be Equally Yoked to transform the circumstance or your sphere of influence.

Where do you land on the CUE Leadership Matrix? What type of leader are you, what would your sphere of influence say about you? How will you close your own gap?

Once you have God's anointing on you, you can:
- operate for the glory of God and nothing else;
- create foundational discipleship and trust in purpose-driven and empowered people;
- change the mechanisms of how something works or is perceived;
- move private and highly visible situations (political, economic, educational, and social) from one condition to the next;
- truly honor others through love; and
- be that indescribable force to bring forth a set of favorable circumstances.

5. Due Season

These favorable set of circumstances, opportunities to serve, or chance to escape bondage have windows. Ecclesiastes 3 tells us that there is a season for everything. Everything has a season, every season has a reason. Sometimes, though, the reason is that we are stupid and we have made bad decisions. Thank God there is a second chance after our mistakes, irrational decisions, regrettable behaviors, and shortcomings.

Our "second chance" has a season. It can be a moment or it can be for a lifetime. But the leader in the mirror has to stay ready, alert, and watchful for the appointed time—your **Due Season**. Due Season is the fifth variable and is the independent variable in the formula. Due Season is not about increase but rather about staying obedient, coping during tough times, and making impact in God's appointed time. The Lord gave Nehemiah the demeanor, perspective, and the words to move Artaxerxes to grant the request to leave as well as protection on the journey and material resources to rebuild Jerusalem. While his people were in despair, Nehemiah served a king who contributed to that despair and the imbalance of Jerusalem's Societal Ecosystem.

Nehemiah was an expert craftsman with unmatched oratory, leadership, facilitation, and coordination skills yet he was a cupbearer for the king. This means he tasted food for a living. This tremendous leader was tasting food. Hmm. And I complained about starting my career in the dirt and grime of a power plant. I chose the cup but then did not want it after I got it. Working shift-work in operations at a coal-fired power plant in far East Texas was not what I had planned for a career. Starting in the mid-90s with a major Texas utility, I thought I would do that for a year or so until Tai graduated. Then we could move to wherever she got accepted to law school. But a year turned to two and to three. I was frustrated about staying in this dead-end role, but the Lord sent a great and dear friend my way to help me cope; Jessie Green. Green, a former star wide receiver at Tulsa, played with the Green Bay Packers and Seattle Seahawks for years in the NFL in the 1970s. He stood about 6'3" and walked with strength and charisma that was hard to ignore. Green was the true definition of an unsung hero. He garnered trust, like, and respect from unions and non-unions alike. From reviewing union contracts to his opinion on how crews should be structured, people wanted his buy-in. It was amazing to watch him interact with others.

Beyond our obvious common skin complexion, our Common Ground was sports and outdoors. How do I describe Green in one word? Committed. He was committed to those he loved and was always consistent. He was always there. If Green gave you his word, you could count on him keeping it at all costs. He poured a lot into me, but most importantly, how to lead people. I learned that no matter the background... I had to find common ground. Green could connect with anyone by finding what was important to them and using it to accomplish something. He was not a politician, for he did not want anything but a person's best in return—never anything for himself. He encouraged me to make my stay worth it and that God had a purpose for me there. Green told me that I needed to discover what that was. Again, he always was looking out for someone else. He was true brother's keeper, biblically speaking.

This was not better displayed than when a few locals decided to hang some lynching nooses, Klan paraphernalia, and literature around

Chapter 9: Transforming the Leader in the Mirror

the plant and in the lockers of some of the black workers. We were told that some white folks were not happy about the hiring of four young black guys. We had heard about the lynching noose, but the black workers who actually received them would not speak up. I had not seen any of it until Green and I stopped by the plant warehouse one afternoon. And there it was—perfectly tied with 13 turns. Wow. Green seemed to transform into someone else. Later, I learned that he was target of small mob in his hometown because he was the first black quarterback ever on his high school football team.

Green asked the warehouse guy why the hangman's noose was hanging at the window for everyone to see? Green did not give the guy a chance to answer, but ordered, "You need to take this down and take it down, now!"

The warehouse guy refused and said that it was not his concern.

Green said, "When I come back here in 20 minutes, this better be gone." When we returned, the noose was still there. Green took out his knife, cut it down, and took to management. On the way to deliver the noose, Green said, "This type of stuff is why I can't leave… I have to ensure that you guys have a chance." Green helped me to cope in a season and bear a cup that I no longer wanted.

How did Nehemiah cope? As Nehemiah experienced, there will tough times in life and, leader in the mirror, you may have to bear a cup that you do not want, like, or feel you deserve. Whether the cup is heavy or light; has a foul smell or sweet aroma; is too hot or cold to handle; is empty or full; or you are trying to balance it while walking in the dark or light; whether you are drinking alone or with a group, you have to bear that cup until God's timing is to release you. We have to maintain readiness and obedience until it is time to be cupbearer no more. Due Season is not about getting your increase… it's not even about getting anything, but rather staying aligned until it is your time to serve or for "things to work for the good for those who love God, those who are called according to His purpose" as Romans 8:28 shares.

For things to work together for the good, remember two key things. Firstly, leader in the mirror, love God; not by mere words but actions that demonstrate that He is your anchor, guiding light, source—your Point of Reverence. In all your ways acknowledge Him (Prov 3:6) at home, alone, at the ballet, at work. Give thanks and

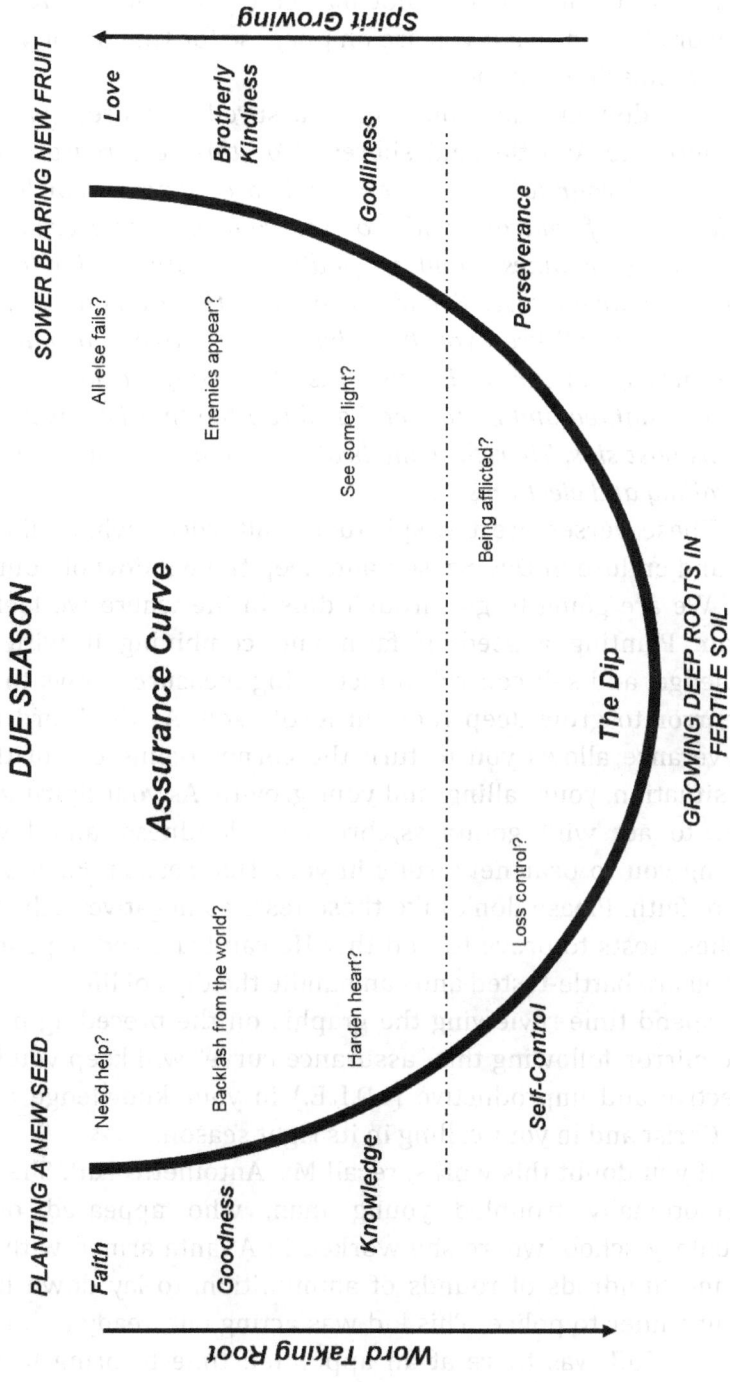

169

Chapter 9: Transforming the Leader in the Mirror

supplication to God. It does not matter where you are. As you have a calling or election, ask if you are on purpose for Him or for yourself with your own mission in mind?

How do you make your calling assured? Let's review 2 Peter 1:5-10, where the Apostle Paul shares, *"For this very reason, make every effort to add your faith, goodness; and to goodness, knowledge; and to knowledge, self-control; and to self-control, perseverance; and to perseverance, godliness; and to godliness, brotherly kindness; and to brotherly kindness, love. For if you possess these qualities in increasing measure, they will keep you from being ineffective and unproductive in your knowledge of our Lord Jesus Christ. But if anyone does not have them, he is near-sighted and blind, and has forgotten that he has been cleansed from his past sins. Therefore, my brothers, be all the more eager to make your calling and election sure."*

These verses are the spiritual healthcheck which allows you to cope and endure in Due Season and keep the window of your anointing open. We are going to go through dips in life where we feel buried in despair. Planting a seed of faith and combining it with goodness, knowledge, and self-control in increasing measure allows the leader in the mirror to grow deep roots in fertile soil. As the Word takes root, perseverance allows you to turn the corner (come out of the dip) on your situation, your calling, and your growth. As your Spirit grows, your ability to act with godliness, brotherly kindness, and love grows… allowing you to bear new fruits in your Due Season. Each of these are tests of faith. Please don't take these tests as negative or blesslessness. Use these tests to prove to God that He can trust and depend on you—that you are battle-tested and can handle the dips of life.

Spend time reviewing the graphic on the preceding page. Leader in the mirror, following this "assurance curve" will keep you from being ineffective and unproductive (I.D.L.E.) in your knowledge of our Lord Jesus Christ and in your calling in its right season.

If you doubt this works, recall Ms. Antoinette Tuff. She persuaded an emotionally troubled young man, who appeared outside the elementary school where she worked in Atlanta armed with an assault rifle and hundreds of rounds of ammunition, to lay down his weapon and surrender to police. This kid was acting out, ready to hurt all in his path. Ms. Tuff was there at an appointed time to bring forth a set of favorable circumstances in the right season for a young man. This young man was the fruit of the Me-Now culture.

Ms. Tuff said, "I was just praying... in the inside of myself and saying 'God, what do I say now? What do I do now?' I just kept saying that on the inside because I knew that I had no words to say."

Tuff later confessed to the 911 dispatcher at the end of the stand-off, "I've never been so scared in all the days of my life. Oh, Jesus."

That was Ms. Tuff's day, her season to be transformational, to walk into her calling. She used every quality in 2 Peter 1:5-10 to cope with the situation and to tap into the spiritual health of this child. She was even a human shield for him. Her second chance did not start that day. It was a result of years of obedience and perfecting holiness—being on accord with God. Leader in the mirror, you can miss your season if you are not ready or not in obedience or are not in proper order. Sometimes in life, we must bear a cup that we don't want. We have to make due with our circumstances whether at a job, home, classroom, church, or in relationships.

Since God has a purpose for each of us, would He not keep that promise if you choose Him? Since God keeps His promises, what happens when you do not keep yours? What happens to an unfulfilled purpose? Here is the thing... No one else can get or take what the Lord has in store for you, only you can miss it, if you do not start and do not obey. The questions now are: Has your purpose left you? Has God's purpose for you passed through your hands like it passed from Saul to David and like it passed from Moses to Joshua? Neither one of them got a second chance to get "in perfect harmony with first order of things via an indescribable force to bring forth a set of favorable circumstances in the right season."

People get second chances. I got multiple chances after running from God on the road to Mt. Zion. The Lord will take the least of us—thief, drug addict, abuser, business owner, liar, a father, a teacher, a preacher, you. He can raise the most dysfunctional to become transformational.

Following the formula: Point of Reverence, Identity, Purpose, Anointing, Due Season, gets you on CUE with God's will, on CUE with His calling on your life (your purpose), and gets others on CUE with that purpose. The Lord will convict you to stay on purpose, to break the

Chapter 9: Transforming the Leader in the Mirror

traditional mode of operation of any situation, to change the inner mechanisms of a situation for His good, to evolve perspectives, to empower people with a driven purpose, and He will navigate you through tests of faith. He will give you a second chance.

When you look at your reflection, what do you see? If you can stand and look in the mirror today, then it's not too late for you to have a second chance. Set aside that which is self-made and begin today leading as God made you. Leader in the mirror, God needs you in the gap created by our Me-Now culture. We need new Shepherds to change the game and shift the momentum and Gatekeepers to stand apost for the sake of this and future generations.

CUE Leadership© Reference Charts

CUE LEADERSHIP MATRIX©

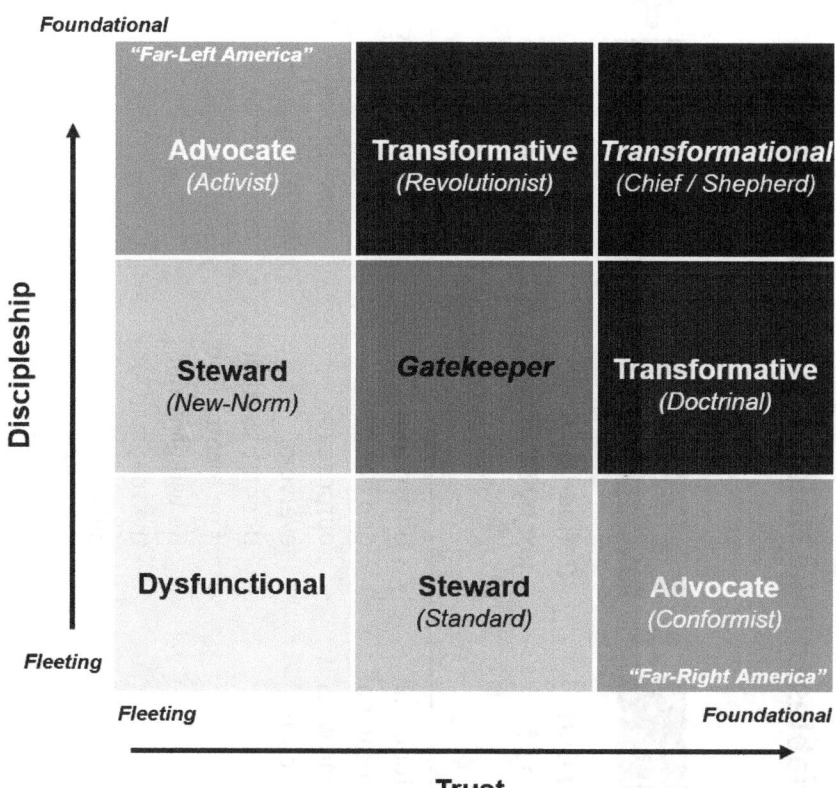

One you have identified the type of leadership you currently demonstrate, CUE Leadership provides tools to move you toward becoming a transformational leader, equipped to shepherd those the Lord puts in your path.

© 2010 CUE Foundation, Inc.

5 Variables to Take Hold of Your Second Chance

	Reverence Point +	Identity +	Purpose +	Anointing +	Due Season
Variables	God as the Point of Reverence	Given by God not by self	Defined by God not by society	Appointed by the Almighty	There is a season for everything
Nehemiah	• Stopped, wept, fasted, prayed • Offered reverence • Confessed sins • Asked God to remember His promise • Asked for favor	• Understood that creation can not determine what it is created for	• Understood that God has a purpose for everyone • Understood that if he locates God, He will give him the roadmap, or gifts	• Knew that staying near to Him grants Divine favor • Knew that God would put a hedge around him	• Maintained readiness and obedience until it was time to be a cupbearer no more

© 2010 CUE Foundation, Inc.

Eric J. Powell Bio

Servant, husband, and father, Eric J. Powell has a calling to inspire and equip all to "lead where they are" and to transform challenges that warp today's society. Eric is married to his college sweetheart, Tai Pentecoste. They have two daughters, Kennedy and Karson, and reside in the Dallas-Fort Worth area.

Honored with the God-granted words and experiences (success, failure, observation, service, and inspiration), Eric formed CUE© Leadership (http://cueleadership.com/) to help leaders from all walks of life to understand there is a higher calling on their lives, to get on one accord with God, and to equip them to walk in that purpose.

As a part of the ministry, Eric coaches adult and youth leaders from all walks of life and hosts a weekly online radio show, onCUE! Radio, which highlights everyday leaders who are making a difference in society. Frequent speaker to industry and community leaders, Eric has authored and co-authored a number of articles, publications, and blogs. He serves the community in other ways including as a current or past board member of several service, arts, and faith-based institutions in the Dallas-Fort Worth area and across the country.

Eric is a Founding Partner & Director of a boutique management consulting firm, where he advises executives, boards, investors, and policymakers in critical market, investment, operational, and infrastructure decisions. Marrying industry, investments, and consulting, he has almost 20 years of experience across many industries, mostly in the energy and infrastructure space. He leads strategy and M&A as well as major corporate change and transformation efforts, where leaders are truly the pivot point of success or failure.

Native of Greenville Alabama, Eric holds a bachelor of science in mathematics from Jacksonville State University in Alabama, where he was an NCAA scholarship athlete and a starring running back on the 1992 Division II National Championship Football team. Black-belt trained, he is certified in Lean Business Operations through the University of Michigan, Ross School of Business.

CUE Leadership©

CUE Leadership Institute is on mission to help leaders of all walks of life to unlock their ability to be transformational, either for a moment or season. Combining biblical principles, corporate transformation experience, and their season and purpose, founder Eric Powell helps corporate, faith-based, and athletic leaders (new or seasoned) to close their gaps, either their own or collective team.

Starting with our ***CUE360 Leadership Diagnostic***, we integrate leadership development, decision-making, and team building through executive coaching, leadership development, and teambuilding in our ***Huddles*** utilizing...

CUE Leadership *(Second Chance)*—Equip leaders in faith-based organizations in taking that second chance to close the gaps

Gatekeeper—Equip young leaders (under 18 years old) to *stand apost* in today's society and emerge as future leaders that educate young leaders in the 3Ls...
- ***Learn*** *about themselves, situations, and people*
- ***Lend*** *talents, time, and treasure in service to others, i.e., being a brother's keeper*
- ***Lead*** *in purpose and in service*

P.L.A.Y! *(Purpose|Leadership|Accountability|You!)*—Develop personalized P.L.A.Y!-books for players, coaches, and supporting staff
- *...understand and fulfill their **purpose***
- *...inspire, build, and equip them with **leadership** development*
- *...ensure **accountability** via decision-making and team building*
- *...breakout Huddle with **your** personalized leadership P.L.A.Y!-book*

Tribe Builder—Build and align the right team (capabilities, roles, and accountability) to support the building, the saving, and the success of your vision and transformational efforts.

To connect with author Eric Powell and CUE Leadership programs visit www.cueleadership.com.

 Thank you for reading *Leader in the Mirror*. We invite you to take the next step in your leadership journey by scanning the QR Code and kindly completing the survey.

If you enjoyed this book, visit www.TouchPublishingServices.com
for more inspiring, challenging, and life-changing books.

Captured Moments

This book contains stories of many wonderful people who have been on this journey with me over the years. I want to share some of my photos with you, to give you a peek at the faces I love.

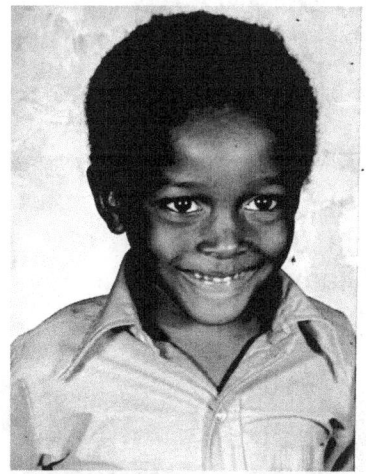

Me in kindergarten

Me (right) with Jody

Two of the Fox Boys - Bobby Joe (center) and Poo-Bear (right). Also pictured is Gene, wife of another Fox Boy, Keno.

The Powell kids, Easter 1978
front row from left: Donna, Jody, me
back row: Shari, Tom III, Gladys, Patricia
not pictured: Sheila

The Powell kids grown up
from left: Donna, Jody, Tom III, Gladys, me, Sheila, Patricia, Shari

Me, running the ball at JSU

With Pops at my graduation

The Powell grandchildren at Mom and Dad's 50th Anniversary

Me (far right) with my brothers:
Tom (center) and Jody

Grandparents' 60th Wedding Anniversary
front: Hugh Mack and Eva Peagler
back: (from left) Mom, Aunt Doris, Aunt Leola, Uncle Hugh

Family photo at our wedding
from left: Shari, Nikia, Gladys, Mother Trish, Maria (Tai's sister), Tai, Ishmaiah, me, Dad, Mom, Genesis, Nancy, Tom

My girls (from left): My daughter Karson, my wife Tai, and my daughter Kennedy

Tai, Kennedy, and I at my parents' 50th wedding anniversary

Me hosting onCUE! Radio

My family in Washington, DC at the 2013 Inauguration

Walking in Washington, DC inspired me to write "Presidential Work-Out"

My parents: Mr. and Mrs. Tommie Powell, Jr. celebrating their 50th wedding anniversary

CPSIA information can be obtained at www.ICGtesting.com
Printed in the USA
LVOW01s2259090215

426297LV00002B/3/P